The CIVIL WAR REENACTORS' ENCYCLOPEDIA

Federal forage cap with regimental insignia and patent air vent in the crown.

The CIVIL WAR REENACTORS' ENCYCLOPEDIA

William C. Davis

ABOVE: Confederate brogans.

LEFT: A very colourful, all-action reenactment of the Battle of McPherson's Ridge, Gettysburg.

SALAMANDER

A SALAMANDER BOOK

Published by
Salamander Books Ltd.
8 Blenheim Court
Brewery Road
London N7 9NT
United Kingdom

© Salamander Books Ltd., 2002

A member of Chrysalis Books plc

ISBN 1 84065 360 4

All rights reserved. Except for use in a review, no part of this book may be reproduced, stored in a retrieval system or transmitted in any form or by any means, electronic, mechanical, photocopying or otherwise, without prior permission of Salamander Books Ltd.

All correspondence concerning the content of this volume should be addressed to Salamander Books Ltd.

CREDITS

PROJECT MANAGER: Ray Bonds

DESIGNER: Mark Holt

COMMISSIONED PHOTOGRAPHY: Don Eiler

UNIFORM ARTWORK: Jeff Burn

BATTLEFIELD MAPS: Jeff Burn and Julian Baker

COLOR REPRODUCTION: Anorax Imaging Ltd

PRINTED IN TAIWAN

THE EDITOR AND CONTRIBUTORS

WILLIAM C. DAVIS has written more than thirty books on American history, particularly on the Civil War period, including two that have achieved Pulitzer Prize nominations. He has acted as consultant and advisor to many organizations including the Eastern National Parks & Monuments Association, the U.S. Intelligence Historical Society, and the N.O.A.A. He graduated as a Master of Arts in History from Sonoma State College, Rohnet Park, California, is a Fellow of the U.S. Army Military History Institute, and the Royal Photographic Society, Bath, England, and an Honorary Doctor of Human Letters, Lincoln Memorial University, Harrogate, Tn. He is Professor of History and Director of Programs for the Virginia Center for Civil War Studies at Virginia Tech.

RUSS A. PRITCHARD, JR., is a graduate of The Choate School, Wallingford, CT, and Washington and Lee University, Lexington, Va. He was Executive Director of the Civil War Library and Museum from 1976 until 1995 and was Technical Advisor for the Civil War trilogy published by Salamander Books, and four other Salamander titles of historical interest. He is retired and resides in Tennessee and Mississippi and serves as a firearms consultant to Conestoga Auction Company, Manheim, Pa.

W. C. SMITH, III, is a consultant for South Carolina State Museum, South Carolina Confederate Relic Room Museum, and Fairfield County Museum. He has been a War Between the States reenactor in Company H, 20th South Carolina Infantry (C.S.), and Company C, 13th United States Infantry (U.S.), and a volunteer living historian at Fort Sumter National Battlefield Monument.

ACKNOWLEDGMENTS

The publishers are grateful to the following individuals and organizations that have provided illustrations and/or artifacts for use in this book, including:

INSTITUTIONAL COLLECTIONS:
The Civil War Library and Museum, Philadelphia, Pa.; The Museum of the Confederacy, Richmond, Va.; the Virginia Historical Society, Richmond, Va.; Virginia Military Institute, Lexington, Va.; West Point Museum, West Point, N.Y.; Chester County Historical Society, West Chester, Pa.; Gettysburg Museum of The Civil War, Gettysburg, Pa.; Milwaukee Public Museum, Milwaukee WI.; The Union League of Philadelphia, Pa.; U.S. Army Ordnance Museum, Aberdeen Proving Ground, Md.; U.S. Army Quartermaster Museum, Fort Lee, Va.

PRIVATE COLLECTIONS:
Guy Leister, Sunbury, Pa.; William LePard, Ardmore, Pa.; Russ A. Pritchard, Mississippi; Mort Sork, Gladwyne, Pa., David Stewart, New Hope, Va.; Donald R. Tharpe, Midland, Va.; Don Troiani, Couthbury CT.; Bob Walter, Arlington Heights, Ill.; John G. Griffiths, Fredericksburg, Pa.; William L. Leugh, III, Chantilly, Va.; Wendell Lang, Tarrytown, NY.; William Smith, Boonsboro, Md.; J. Craig Nannos, Ardmore, Pa.; Benjamin P. Michel, Millburn, N.J.; George Lomas, Hatboro, Pa.; Michael J. McAfee, West Point, N.Y.; CDR James C. Reurmund, USN (Ret), F.R.N.S, Richmond, Va.

PHOTOGRAPHERS AND PHOTOGRAPH LIBRARIES:
Don Eiler of Don Eiler's Custom Photography, Richmond, Va., for the vast majority of excellent artifact photographs in this book; Anne and Rolf Lang, of Arlington, Va., for all the reenactment photographs shown; Robert Clasby, of Historic Graphics, for his battlefield reconstruction artwork on page 22; and the National Archives and Library of Congress for the many contemporary photographs reproduced here.

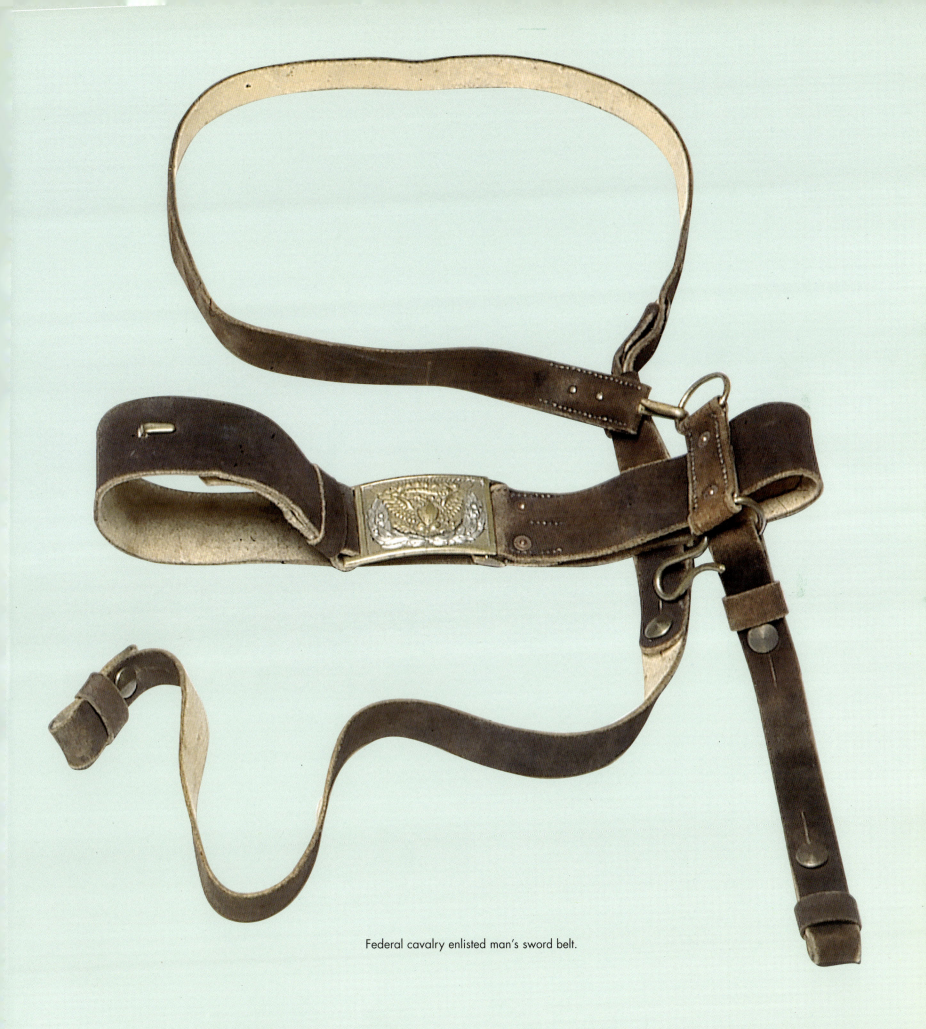
Federal cavalry enlisted man's sword belt.

CONTENTS

FOREWORD
~ 8 ~

REENACTING THE WAR BETWEEN THE STATES
~ 14 ~

UNIFORMS, WEAPONS AND EQUIPMENT
~ 32 ~

EQUIPMENT OF THE FEDERAL FORCES
~ 38 ~

EQUIPMENT OF THE CONFEDERATE FORCES
~ 126 ~

THE BATTLES
~ 188 ~

INDEX
~ 252 ~

LEFT: 'Confederate' soldiers preparing to march on 'McPherson's Ridge', during the 1999 reenactment of actions during the Battle of Gettysburg.

Foreword by William C. Davis

Just as archaeologists can discern much of a long-gone culture's daily life and history from the remains left behind, so can those who would learn more of the daily lives and experiences of the Civil War soldiers glean much just from knowing more about the physical environment in which those men functioned, and especially from the items that made up the catalog of their personal belongings and accouterments during the war. Their weapons tell us how they fought, as well as lesser things like the weight they had to carry on the march, the taste in their mouths in battle when they had to bite into their cartridges to load their guns, and even the smells of their campsite as they oiled and cleaned them. Their uniforms reveal much of their degree of comfort: how warm or cold they were in the climates in which they fought; how prone their clothing may have been to lice and fleas; how much their movement was free or restricted. And the equipment they carried affords insights into their daily lives, their simple pleasures, and their attitude toward themselves and their armies. There is an old saying that if you would know a man, you must first walk a mile in his shoes. Well, Johnny Reb and Billy Yank walked thousands of miles in their gear, and to know those soldiers we need to know what they were wearing and carrying as they trudged all those weary miles.

Only militarist totalitarian nations are ever really prepared for war when it erupts. Democratic nations, almost by definition, are caught, if not by surprise, then at least unready for the clash of arms when it comes. Such was the case with the United States when it split into two democracies in 1860-1861. Indeed, at the outset, armed forces in the new Confederate States of America briefly outnumbered those in the old Union prior to the first shots at Fort Sumter, and some of them were probably better armed, since they were largely privately raised volunteers equipped at their own expense with the latest

BELOW: The "spit and polish" that marked the fighting man, North and South, early in the war disappeared on the long marches, and well before the major battles. For the reenactor, to have walked with these men in their new uniforms, and with all items of kit present and correct, would have been instructive, and even more interesting with those who survived.

arms and equipment. On the other hand, however, other "Southrons" were state militia armed with whatever happened to be in the state armories, some of it up to date, and some almost antediluvian.

A soldier's weapon in this war would be his least used article of equipment, for the average soldier spent only one day in twenty in actual combat, yet most men in the ranks would consider it their most essential article. It is ironic, then, that at the war's outset, and for more than a year afterward, the armament of the common soldiers would be chaotic at best, even for the Union.

By 1861 the United States Army had standardized its infantry weapon on a couple of recent patterns of rifled percussion shoulder arms manufactured at its armories at Springfield, Massachusetts, Harpers Ferry, Virginia, and elsewhere. It had settled on the .58 caliber as representing the best combination of power and mass with efficiency, and virtually all of its obsolete Mexican War era smoothbore muskets had been retired, sold, or given to state militias, some in the South. But with only 16,000 enlisted men on the books as of April 1861, and with only about 13,000 actually on duty, the North would need vastly greater quantities of weapons as its army grew almost overnight to 100,000, and then rapidly to nearly a million. And of course, its need for arms was even greater since the capture of arsenals in the South meant that much of its store of spare weapons was lost at a stroke.

Contracts would go out to private manufacturers to supply as much as was possible, while the government armories worked overtime. Even that was not sufficient, and large supplies of guns were purchased abroad from Austria, Belgium, and other nations, and especially the Enfield rifle from Great Britain, with its .577 caliber virtually compatible with the United States standard. Union cavalry would carry mostly breechloading carbines, as well as pistols, most often the Colt .44 caliber revolver. While

BELOW: After all the marching, drill, drill and more drill was not just for the sake of tidiness, but for operational competence. This light artillery battery would have drilled several times a day before going into combat.

whole regiments were armed with breechloading arms, the predominant weapon remained the muzzleloading rifle-musket.

For the Confederates, by contrast, the chaos was epidemic. As young men rushed to enlist, with state arsenals soon exhausted and the new Confederate government as yet unfunded and with no facilities for manufacturing of its own, volunteers simply brought whatever they had at home with them. Regiments hurried to the front with shotguns, common rifles, Mexican War percussion and flintlock muskets, and some men even carried earlier smoothbore longarms and old flintlock Tennessee, Pennsylvania, or Kentucky hunting rifles. The calibers represented every number imaginable, from miniscule .24 up to whopping .75 caliber killers. In time the Confederacy would itself buy large quantities of rifled longarms, mostly Pattern 1853 Enfields, from England and other countries, augmenting what it was able to capture from United States arsenals and from battlefields, and even limited home grown manufacturing concerns. And in time it would standardize its infantry arms on the .58 model too, though many regiments also carried .69s. Confederate cavalrymen preferred carbines and .44 caliber pistols when they could get them, but in the end the Southern horsemen used whatever they were given.

The Union would always enjoy greater firepower, more reliable weapons, and greater availability of replacements for lost or worn out rifles, but still by 1865 even the South had more weapons than it had men to carry them. Meanwhile edged weapons like swords, bayonets, and knives, represented an even greater variety of sizes, styles, and makes. The South, again, had to make do with what it could buy or what was already on hand. Some officers went to war with their fathers' or grandfathers' swords from

RIGHT: Heavily armed he may appear in this pose, but this Johnny Reb would soon find that his U.S. Model 1855 single-shot pistol with carbine shoulder stock was quickly superseded, and he would have little use for the two Colt Navy .36 caliber poistols in his belt.

FAR RIGHT: This unknown Union cavalryman, like tens of thousands of his kind, swept across the war-torn country and into legend. He poses with his saber, his Sharps carbine, and his Colt Model 1860 Army revolver in .44 caliber.

RIGHT: Men of Co. I, believed to be a unit of 12th New York, and including some Zouaves, relax in their relatively smart attire. Some wear havelocks made for them by patriotic women. These white kepis with long tails were touted as sure-fire preventives of sunstroke. Wearers soon found that they cut off circulation of air around the head and face, so they did what they did with the neck socks – dumped them.

earlier wars. Enlisted men brought Bowie knives and dirks and daggers from home, and some infantrymen went the whole war without a bayonet, or depended on getting one from a fallen comrade or a killed or captured Yankee. In the North, of course, the situation was dramatically better. Every infantryman had a bayonet, based on only a couple of established patterns, and officers and cavalrymen had regulation swords made in abundance either at government armories or else by contracted manufactures.

If the cacophony of weapons was dazzling, how much more so was the infinite variety of uniforms. Indeed, well into the war there were so many, of such varying design and color, that often men and even commanders could not tell at a glance whether a regiment in the near distance was friend or foe. In the beginning, in North and South alike, there was a host of local private and county militia organizations, many of which had existed as social and fraternal groups for years before the war. State militia usually had standard uniform clothing, though in the North it was often gray, and in the South it was just as often blue. The private units bought or made whatever they wanted. Some wore green. Others adopted the Zouave uniform of baggy pants, short coattee, and leggings, topped off by a fez or even a turban, and in colors ranging from gaudy reds to stripes in blue and white, much of it covered with ornate gold "frogging" or braid. No wonder there was often confusion on the battlefield.

Rather quickly, however, both sides moved toward standardization. In the North it would be a dark blue wool blouse or jacket with matching hat, either a French style kepi, or the high-crowned

Hardee or Jeff Davis hat, over light blue trousers. Even the Zouave regiments soon adopted the standard issue when their colorful garb wore out, for the government would not replace such special clothing. By 1865, the only real differentiation in Union uniforms were the colors of rank insignia based on branch of service. Soldiers in the Western or Trans-Appalachian theater of the war tended to wear baggier sack coats and slouch hats, while those in the East conformed more to the regulations.

In the South, meanwhile, the efforts at standardization inevitably met with less success. Jefferson Davis soon established "cadet gray" as the official color for Confederate uniforms, mostly in cotton, but the difficulty in obtaining dyes meant that often substitutes had to be used. As a result, many soldiers actually wore a gray that was closer to a light blue, while others were in shades of brown called "butternut." Fortunate was the Rebel who had a complete uniform at any one time, and when clothing wore out there were often no replacements, so that the Confederate soldier often represented a mixture of government issue, homespun clothes brought from home, and what could be bought or captured from Yankees along the way. Indeed, in photos of groups of Confederate soldiers taken late in the war, it is difficult to distinguish them from any crowd of civilian men. Even boots and shoes were a problem, and not a few Confederates spent substantial parts of their service essentially barefoot.

There were certain articles that every soldier needed to have, both for his subsistence as a man, and his efficiency as a fighter. Beside his weapons, he needed a leather belt and on it a cap box for the percussion caps that fired his weapon, and a box for his cartridges – tubes of paper wrapped around the base of a bullet and a charge of powder. Ideally there should be a sling or scabbard for his bayonet, too. Over his shoulder he slung a haversack to carry his rations and his few personal items like toothbrush, reading material, candles, and such, and/or a knapsack on his back for more personal articles, with his blanket roll and his half of a two-man shelter tent rolled on top.

This was the ideal, and thousands of volunteers in 1861 and 1862 went off to war so equipped from the North. But they quickly learned what to keep and what to discard so as to lighten their load, and by late in the war few Yankee soldiers would be seen on the march with all of that impedimenta. As for the Confederates, most of them simply never had it in the first place. They, too, required at least the belt and cap and cartridge boxes, although as leather became scarce not a few just carried their ammunition in their pockets. Bayonet scabbards were often not needed since some Rebels never got bayonets, while others – like their Northern counterparts – developed a disdain for their bayonets as essentially useless, and discarded or gave them away. As for the rest of the kit, knapsacks soon wore out, and most Confederate soldiers were never supplied with them in the first place. They relied on haversacks, which were easier for the government to make and issue, or even on sacks or carpetbags brought from home. Tent sections, or "flies," were another luxury, and often as not the Southern soldier simply rolled all his worldly goods inside his blanket and then slung it over one shoulder and across his chest and tied the ends together at his waist.

What the soldiers carried with them varied widely, but there were usually a few basic items to be found in any knapsack or haversack, North or South. A sewing kit or "housewife," as it was called. A pipe and tobacco. A bible or New Testament. Perhaps some of the religious and moral tracts handed out in the camps by *colporteurs*, as a counterbalance to the decks of cards and semi-pornographic French prints and photographs often found in the same knapsacks. Letters from home, and paper and pen or pencil if the soldier was literate. Books were few because they were heavy, but there might be a copy of a recent newspaper, and certainly there would be *carte-de-visite* photographs of a loved one at home, especially a wife and children or a special lady friend.

The Yankee soldier had an advantage perhaps even greater than his initial superiority in his equipment, for when it was lost, worn out, or discarded in battle and not found afterward, it could all be replaced, and usually within a reasonable time. Southern manufacturing and purchasing simply never could keep pace with the wear and tear of camp and campaign, which only put added strains on the well worn pockets in gray and butternut trousers that were themselves worn thin to near-transparency. With holes in his shoes, holes in his clothing, holes in his pockets, and little enough to put in them in the first place, Johnny Reb was scarcely equipped for basic subsistence, let alone fighting a war.

RIGHT: Soldiers both North and South carried small personal items in their knapsacks, often to remind them of home. Those shown here were the property of Henry L. Dempsey, a Union soldier who was held in the notorious Andersonville prison for over a year, although he survived the war. They include (top left) a "housewife," a night cap, eating uternsils, a bible given to him by his mom, and photos of his brothers John and James, both of whom were killed in action.

Reenacting the War Between the States

By W. C. Smith, III

ABOVE: Forage cap of Lieutenant Colonel William Fowler, 146th New York Regiment.

LEFT: Fabulous reenactment of Pickett's Charge, during the Battle of Gettysburg, one of the most dramatic actions of the Civil War.

Reenacting the War Between the States

The men of Kershaws's Brigade of South Carolinians, part of The Army of Northern Virginia, march shoulder to shoulder in line of battle, their weapons at shoulder arms. It's the second day of the Battle of Gettysburg, 2 July 1863, and the Confederate troops are grimy, tired, and more than a little afeared. As they march across a wheat field, they step over the dead and dying, ignoring the desperate cries for water in the summer heat. Their eyes are wide and their teeth clinched as they scan the scene in front of them. As they cross through an abandoned Federal artillery battery, the guns now attended by the dead of the Federal Army of the Potomac, a feeling of being alone grips them. The roar of the guns seems to dull into a constant thud. The smoke and the clouds of dirt mix to form an orange glow to the sky that envelops the scene all around.

There before them, not more than thirty paces away, stands a wall of blue men and glittering steel centered on the colors of the Union. The Confederate troops are fixed on the sight. They cannot afford even to blink for fear of the sight changing.

For what seems like only a moment the troops really feel they are present on that long-silent battlefield, sensing the smell of gunpowder, dirt, sweat, and horses. However, it is not 2 July 1863. It is in fact late June 1988, at the 125th Anniversary reenactment of the Battle of Gettysburg. This is my moment, the moment all reenactors strive for, the moment they step through a portal in time to stand in history. This moment is fleeting and some reenactors capture it only once in their time in the hobby, but it is worth all the sacrifice to reach it.

RIGHT: Reenactors aim for realism, in action and attire and equipment. When successful they can really get the sense of "being there," of having relived a historic occasion.

BELOW: The clattering of arms, the roar of firearms, the smell of discharged black powder, the whoops of defiance from Johnny Reb or Billy Yank, really bring the big events, such as this Gettysburg reenactment, to life.

BELOW RIGHT: A formidable sight as the warriors line up against each other, just as they did in the Battle of Gettysburg, July 1-3, 1863. Casualties were high on those terrible three days; when the battle was over both sides had lost a fourth of their armies.

Taking up the hobby of what is known as War Between the States Reenacting is not a decision to take lightly. It is demanding of your time, money, and physical and mental capabilities. While age is not an important factor, one needs to be reasonably fit. Reenactment events occur during all kinds of weather and temperatures. To fully experience them you must be willing to live in a tent or in the open at an event, march endlessly, drill often, wear wool when it is one hundred degrees, and eat like soldiers did at the time. You cannot expect to stay in a hotel and live out of a cooler and experience the life of the 1860s soldier. Many who ascribe to the hobby try to include these modern conveniences and most of them just look forward to the battle reenactments as an opportunity to burn powder and shoot at Yanks or Rebs. But if you really want to relive history, to truly relive the period you are trying to portray, that is not the direction in the hobby that you should take.

Reenacting is an expensive hobby. Like everything else in life you only get out of it what you are willing to put into it. Yes, you can save money by making some of your accouterments, and by buying used uniforms and equipment, but you still must make that initial investment required just to set foot on the field, not to mention travel expenses to get to events. If you want to try it out first to see if you like the hobby, most reenactment units you may join can provide your basic needs to attend an event. Do not expect them, however, to keep you outfitted on "loaners" for a long period of time. They will expect you to abide by the uniform and equipment guidelines of the group and to contribute to the organization with an accurate portrayal of what the members of the group represent.

Reenacting the War Between the States

BELOW: Reenacting is not merely an occasion for Yank and Reb to take shots at each other, to relive the physical and political conflict. Behind any vainglory lies a deeper message that no human experience is more personal or traumatic than a battle: when men go into battle, each soldier goes on his own, acutely aware that his may be one of the lives lost.

Reenacting can also be very time consuming. But you must not let the hobby consume all of your time; if you allow it to it will. Remember, it is just a hobby, not a lifestyle. With that in mind, however, bear in mind that the group you may belong to will have some expectations of your time contribution to the group's efforts.

You may ask, "Why even join a group?" While it is not as demanding on your time to freelance as a reenactor, it is difficult to just show up at an event and fall in with a group. You must obtain members' permission and meet their expectations in your appearance and drill. This type of participation in the hobby could be more expensive, since you would have to have a wide range of equipment to maintain several historical impressions so as to be able to fit in at a moment's notice. As a freelance it would be best to establish a relationship with several groups and try to be included in the ranks of one of them prior to an event you wish to attend, rather than just showing up. This could save you much time and effort at the event. Indeed, in many reenactments (and in all of the big ones) it is a requirement that reenactors be officially associated with a specific group if they wish to take part.

All this considered, is War Between the States reenacting the hobby for you? If you love to read the history of the war, enjoy the study of the weapons, uniforms, and equipment that were carried into battle, want to experience what it was like to live as a soldier at the time, enjoy sharing your knowledge of the times with the public through living history, enjoy the outdoors and the company of others of kindred interest, then this is the best avenue to satisfy your passion and interest in this period in American history.

It is important to understand the history of the War Between the States reenacting hobby itself before getting involved. The seeds of the hobby were planted in May 1950 when two five-man teams armed with .58 caliber rifle-muskets paraded in the rain at the Berwyn Rod and Gun Club in Muirkirk, Maryland. They wore period-styled uniforms and fired live volleys at two groups of fifteen balloons. At that moment the North-South Skirmish Association was born. The NSSA can today boast of over 200 teams and more than 3,500 members. The NSSA's purpose is to conduct what it calls skirmishes (organized target competition using muzzle-loading weapons in the original manner while wearing Civil War style uniforms) and to encourage the preservation of War Between the States material.

Springing forth from this group and culminating on July 22 and 23, 1961, some 2,000 members of the North-South Skirmish Association and hundreds of volunteers created the first large-scale reenactment of the Battle of Manassas. The 100th Anniversary reenactment was a feature of the Civil War Centennial celebration sponsored by the National Parks Service on the site of the original Battle of 1st Manassas. The Civil War Centennial captured the imagination and attention of the entire nation. Today's reenactment community is no longer associated with the NSSA but owes a great deal to the early NSSA members for establishing the origins of the current hobby of living history.

Today, reenacting has come of age. The reenactments of the 1960s, with their amateurish uniforms and of untrained volunteers, are a thing of the past. The 125th Anniversary battle series between 1986 and 1990 proved that living history had evolved from light-hearted weekends to professionally performed events. Safety and security consciousness was raised at that time, and even the largest event during the 125th Anniversary, Gettysburg 1988, which fielded 12,000 armed men, was executed without any serious accidents reported.

No one should be allowed on the field of a reenactment without the proper training. Every unit should have an officer devoted to monitoring safety at every event. Accidents will occur but reenactments must take steps right down to the individual soldier to make it a safe hobby. Everyone on the field must remember that deaths have occurred, limbs have been lost, and lives have been changed due to some simple careless act in pursuit of the hobby. Alcohol, drugs, and gunpowder do not mix. There are many publications available on black powder safety. Check with your local gun dealer who sells black powder and caps for information. There are strict government regulations involving black powder and caps, so learn the rules and obey them. The *Civil War News*, a publication for the Civil War enthusiast has on its web site, www.civilwarnews.com a very good list of safety procedures for artillery, for instance.

When you have considered the hobby and found that it is of interest to you, you must find a reenactment group with which to become associated. It is recommended that you attach yourself to a group as a new member of the hobby. This will give you the training and drill instruction necessary to get your feet on the ground. To find the right group ask yourself what you want to portray, Union,

Reenacting the War Between the States

Confederate, or both; infantry, cavalry, artillery, Navy, Marine, civilian, etc.; or a member of specific unit. Rank is earned in the hobby just like it is in the military of the day, so do not expect to be anything but a private when you start.

Once you have decided on what you want to portray you can check with museums and historical societies for contact details of the local groups. You can also attend a reenactment event and scout the participating groups. One of the best places to search for a unit today is on the internet since many reenactment groups now have their own websites.

When you have made contact, ask a lot of questions. Check them out for the authenticity level and compare it to the authenticity level you wish to achieve in your impression. All groups tend to vary in authenticity, from mainstream reenactors to hardcore living historians. Within the hobby, those who achieve the hardcore title are often called "stitch counters," while those who achieve less than what is required in the mainstream reenacting community are called "farbs" ("far be it from me to question his impression"). You don't want to be a farb. Make sure the group you choose is comfortable for you or you can become frustrated by the group's inability to meet your expectations. While it is most convenient to be a member of a local group you may have to join an out of state group in order to achieve your expectations.

Now begins the search for the right clothing and equipment. During the war the troops were

BELOW: Over more than fifty years reenacting of the War Between the States evolved from its humble target competition beginnings to the great anniversary events in which thousands of individuals played their parts in well-organized and stirring performances.

BELOW RIGHT: At the big events, thunderous cannon roar to delight the spectators, while the participants follow strict procedures to ensure the safety of all parties.

BELOW: With firearms being discharged amid throngs of reenactment participants, there is a huge responsibility for each individual taking part to follow safety guidelines.

BELOW RIGHT: Newly enrolled reenactors can expect to begin their "military careers" as they would in real-life situations: in the rank and file, from which they can progress via promotion.

serviced by traders called sutlers, who sold all sorts of items from the backs of their wagons. It is much the same today, as sutlers follow reenactors and reenactments as well. Modern sutlers sell everything that a reenactor would need to pursue his or her hobby. They set up and sell their wares at all the reenactment events on what is called "sutlers row," a sort of an outdoor reenactors retail mall. Today's sutlers also sell their wares by mail order and on the internet.

Sutlers can be found all over the United States. They travel great distances to visit many reenactments to sell their products. You will need to question experienced reenactors as to the reliability of sutlers concerning authenticity and business practices. Most sutlers are helpful merchants but there are those who just want to make a sale, so "buyer beware."

The unit you have joined will most likely be able to tell you where to go to satisfy their uniform and equipment requirements. Find a reliable member of your group to act as your mentor until you are up to speed. This will be a great advantage when you inevitably have questions, rather than getting ten different answers to the same question.

There are several internet sites you may wish to visit to find answers and to find how to purchase the right equipment and uniforms. One very informative site which will be especially useful for those reenactors interested in the highest levels of authenticity is "The Authentic Campaigner" at www.authentic-campaigner.com. This site can provide you with resources on clothing, equipment,

Reenacting the War Between the States

RIGHT: Keen reenactors strive for authenticity in their apparel and equipment, but the degree of authenticity varies from those who just want to join in the fun up to the "stitch counters" intent on matching even the smallest button to contemporary perfection. Similarly, there are artists who over the years have depicted incidents on the Civil War battlefields when clearly they have no real knowledge of the terrain, or the disposition of forces, but have based their idealistic works on the thrilling accounts in contemporary newspapers or subsequent books, including memoirs of officers whose memories have somewhat dimmed with the passage of time. Not so, however, with the excellent works of Robert Clasby, of Historic Graphics, as shown in this depiction of "the charge of the 1st Minnesota on the second day of Gettysburg," one of a series he is preparing. Robert goes to extraordinary lengths to ensure accuracy. The works are created using hundreds of digital photographs of reenactors blended together using digital imaging techniques. Whenever possible he uses the actual battlefield site for the picture and tries to restore it to its historic look.

groups, publications, and Civil War chat rooms. If your interest is in authentic cavalry horse equipment, such as saddles, the sutler to see can be found on the internet at www.fburgess.com. This company makes some of the finest and most authentic cavalry horse equipment. Mainstream or average reenactors can find most everything they need at the old and reliable sutlers of C&D Jarnagin (www.jarnaginco.com) and Falls Creek Sutlery (www.fcsutler.com). Both of these have provided the reenactment community with high quality, well-made uniforms and equipment for many years.

When considering clothes its best to start from the feet up, because when your feet are unhappy so will you be unhappy. The basic footwear of the War Between the States soldier was the brogan. The U.S. Government issue brogan was a black ankle-high boot with the rough side of the leather turned out, wooden heels, thick leather soles fixed with wooden pegs, and leather shoelaces without metal eyelets. These boots have a left and right foot and should include a metal heel plate and toe plate so as to extend the life and wear of the brogan.

Confederate brogans vary in quality and style from the U.S.-issue boot. One type of Confederate brogan has no left or right foot and is made with the smooth side of the leather out. It has pegged wooden heels and a stitched heavy leather sole. The fact that it doesn't have a defined left and right foot sounds a little uncomfortable, but it is not. In time the shoes will conform to the shape of your feet if you consistently wear them on the same feet. It is advisable to wear heel plates with any Confederate brogan, to extend the life of the boot. There is an advantage to wearing the smooth-side-out boot in a Confederate style as opposed to the U.S.-issue rough-side-out brogan: the smooth-side-out boot repels water better and thereby could last longer than the rough-side-outs.

Thick woolen socks must be worn with your brogans to protect your feet on long marches. It is to your advantage to break in those new brogans before a reenactment event. When new they are like wearing concrete blocks and are so stiff they could easily substitute as a hammer for driving nails. Wear them first around the house, when working in the yard or garden, until they have that field-worn look and become more pliable.

A true authentic reenactor is correct in his dress right down to his underclothes. The 1860s soldier wore under-drawers and shirts made of cotton muslin. The buttons were white, three- and four-hole porcelain. If these types of buttons are not available from your sutler you can often find them in button jars at your local antique shop. Remember, the shirt was considered an undergarment. A man of that period would not be seen in public wearing just a shirt. Coats were worn year round by civilian and military personnel.

In the Confederate Army and in some Union regiments, such as the Garibaldi Guard, a battle shirt was worn when proper uniform coats were not available or when the unit's uniform required it. Battle shirts were large-fitting flannel shirts with voluminous ballooned sleeves. They often had some

RIGHT: The appearance of mounted forces on the reenactment battlefield always creates a stir of excitement for the spectators. Reenactments of McPherson's Ridge, Gettysburg, always bring an element of poignancy, since it was here that the valiant Federal General John F. Reynolds, a local to the area, was struck by a chance bullet from a Rebel gun and died in the saddle.

Reenacting the War Between the States

sort of piping and large pockets. In the Confederate Army the battle shirt was seen most often in the western theater of war.

Military trousers of the time were made of wool, which had a very loose weave to the fabric. Three- and four-hole metal buttons were used on the fly and as suspender buttons. There were no hip pockets, only side pockets and on occasion a watch pocket. The waist of the pants was open in the back and tied or buckled. Other types of material used in trousers were a form of heavy jean material and a combination of wool and cotton called "linsey woolsey."

The reenactor will need to break in new trousers. Wool shrinks, but if carefully hand-washed in cold water and air-dried in a cool place, new trousers will soon acquire a used and comfortable look and feel. Never heat-dry, iron or crease your trousers.

Most War Between the States coats were made of the same fabrics as the trousers and, with the exception of the Federal-issue sack coat, were lined with various materials. As during the war, this lining could be to the reenactor's advantage in hot weather. As you perspire into the lining the dampness can serve to reverse the heat and cool your body.

Hats of the period varied but the soldier of the 1860s, for the most part, wore the forage cap in the Federal Army of the eastern theater, while the broad brim slouch hat was worn by Federal troops in the western theater and by the Confederate Army. The slouch hat, while looking less military than

RIGHT: Whether it was a Federal black ankle-high boot, or Confederate undyed brown leather brogan, or whether they were rough side in or out, the basic footwear of the Civil War soldier would have taken some time to wear in to a comfortable fit. So, too, will it be for the reenactor, who will doubtless be dedicated enough to suffer for his hobby.

RIGHT: Normally, the Civil War period soldier, in uniform or civvies, would always be seen in public with his jacket on, the shirt being considered an undergarment. But when soldiers relaxed around a hot and dusty camp, it was not long before they cooled off in their shirtsleeves.

the forage cap, was better suited to protect its wearer from the elements.

It is for the most part a far simpler task to research the uniforms worn by Federal forces during the war than those worn by Confederate soldiers. With the exception of many early war state units, most Federal regiments were supplied with government-issue uniforms. Even the non-conventional uniforms worn by early Federal troops are well documented, however, and many examples still exist in museums for study. The Smithsonian Institution has created a video tape (*Enlisted Uniforms of the Civil War*) with graphic detail on the styles, cut, and colors of the issue uniforms of the Federal government during the war. In addition there are numerous resources for viewing original photographs of Union soldiers.

The Confederate soldier on the other hand used an endless variety of "uniforms," including civilian dress. There was very little commonality, even among regiments. Uniform cloth was made locally and in England by a multitude of suppliers. Dyes varied from a greenish gray, cadet gray, and brownish gray to many shades of brown called "butternut." The styles of the coats varied by state issue, prewar militia, and issuing government depots. For example, the Richmond depot issued a waistcoat or shell jacket to the Army of Northern Virginia in May 1863 which had a gray fabric with a slight green tint. One year later, that same depot issued to the Army of Northern Virginia a similar-

Reenacting the War Between the States

styled jacket but in a dark, almost black, charcoal gray.

The uniforms, weapons, and equipment shown in these pages are all original items from the Civil War period, photographed in various museums and in privately owned collections. The photographs are intended to inspire reenactors to aspire to as high a level of authenticity as possible when searching for items for their impressions. However, it is recognized that reenactors rarely use authentic items. Almost anything you need for your impression has been reproduced and is available from sutlers. An authentic weapon may be seen on occasion or an authentic item may be used in a living history presentation, but no reenactor in his right mind would risk endangering an historical and valuable artifact.

The best approach to researching what would be appropriate for your impression is to seek out examples worn by the men in the unit you represent at museums and historic societies. Examine photographs of men who served in the unit you are portraying. There are several published sources for Confederate images, including William Albaugh's *Confederate Faces* series of books, William Turner's *Even More Confederate Faces*, and D. A. Serizano's *Still More Confederate Faces*. More resources for photographs include the series *Portraits of Conflict* and, for North Carolina troops, *State Troops and Volunteers* by Greg Mast. Extremely fine books describing and portraying the equipment, conditions, and battles of the Civil War forces have been written by William C. Davis and published as

BELOW: Almost every type of Federal headgear is on display in this line-up of the staff of talented engineer Brigadier (later Major) General Godfrey Weitzel (seated, center), who helped plan the defenses of Cincinnati and Washington, and became Maj. Gen. Benjamin F. Butler's chief engineer. In this late 1862 photo the men are also displaying a wide variety of jackets and coats.

RIGHT: Among the best resources for reenactors in search of authentic apparel and equipment are contemporary photographs, those of men of the North being more readily available than those of the South. Here, Lieutenant Parker of the Union's 4th Michigan poses with two of his soldiers and possibly his body servant.

FAR RIGHT: Some of the better photographs of Southern soldiers were taken by Northern photographers! This one, believed to have been made by Mathew Brady, shows the dashing "Gray Ghost," John Singleton Mosby of Virginia, a Confederate colonel who led the 43rd Virginia Partisan Rangers on many successful raids behind enemy lines, and captured two Yankee generals.

a trilogy by Salamander Books (*Fighting Men*, *Commanders*, and *Battlefields of the Civil War*). Another excellent source for color photographs of original Union and Confederate uniforms is *Army Blue* by John Langellier and the Time Life Books, *Echoes of Glory*. The Union and Confederate uniform system is well explained and illustrated in *American Civil War Confederate Army* by Ron Field and *Civil War Uniforms* by Smith and Field. Manuals such as *Hardee's Tactics* and the *U.S. Army Regulations of 1861* have even been published in simpler versions that even modern man can understand. Authentic sutlers have already done a great deal of research and can be of help during your search for the right impression.

The types of leather accouterments and equipment available vary only in authentic quality. For example most sutlers who provide leather goods can come up with an adequately functioning cartridge box, but there are some sutlers who deal in reproduction cartridge boxes that are authentic in every detail. The sutlers study authentic examples in private collections and museums and through practice and trial and error reproduce the original for use by the reenacting community. Naturally, the more authentic the piece the more you will have to pay for it. Quality costs. This adage applies to all uniforms and equipment offered by sutlers. You must study the requirements of your group.

Federal-issue leather accouterments are fairly standard and vary only by model, whereas Confederate leather accouterments can vary a great deal. As an example let's look at waist belts.

Reenacting the War Between the States

BELOW: Authentic items that would have been found in a Confederate soldier's knapsack include those cared for and displayed by The Civil War Library and Museum, Philadelphia, Pa., together with some loaned by the J. Craig Nannos Collection. Such displays, and photographs, are typical of the rich source of references for the reenactor, who would be looking for well-made facsimiles, since no one would take such valuable and often fragile artifacts into a battle reenactment.

Confederate waist belts were not made to any government standard. They were made and sold to the government or state by a multitude of manufacturers, including back-yard leather works. Belts varied in width, color, belt plate or buckle and material. When leather was in short supply some "leather" accouterments were even made of heavy canvas material. At the other end of the scale, the finest in Confederate-used leather accouterments were imported through the blockade from England. Again, sutlers today can provide a wide range of the accouterments at every level of authentic quality, including copies of the English-made examples.

Of special interest in the area of equipment for every reenactor will be a canteen. An excellent study of canteens can be found in the book *Civil War Canteens* by Steve Sylvia and Michael O'Donnell. Federal-issue canteens were limited to the Model 1858 smooth-side canteen and bullseye canteen. Both were made of tin with a pewter spout, and both were covered with wool in various shades, and had a cotton sling. These excellent canteens were prized by the Confederate soldier as well. The only drawback to the 1858-style canteen, including those supplied today, is that the interiors of the canteens tend to rust and cause the water to take on an interesting orange color. Not to worry though, during a hot battle reenactment you will drink almost anything and no one has become sick from the orange water yet. You will note that in many photos of troops in the field the wool covers seem to be missing. Today, as then, they make great patching material for wool uniforms and also

serve other purposes as well.

If you are a Confederate reenactor and wish to use the classic wood canteen it is important to coat the inside of the canteen with wax, since wood swells and contracts when wet and leaks will occur. The other classic Confederate canteen, the tin drum type, comes with no cover or pewter spout but is still a very good water container. Its only drawbacks are again the orange-colored water and its small size. The small size prevents you from carrying as much water as the 1858 Federal canteen can hold; this would be a disadvantage on the long march, as it was during the war.

The Civil War style bedroll is made up of a wool blanket and a rubberized canvas blanket, which serves several purposes. At night it is to be placed on the ground under you, rubberized side down, to separate you from the damp ground. It can also be used to wrap your wool blanket in when on the march to prevent rain getting onto it. It can also double as a rain poncho or shelter.

Your bayonet can also have many functions other than its prime one as a weapon, such as pot hook and candle holder. In fact, most of your equipment can serve multiple practical uses to make living in the outdoors more comfortable. Necessity is the mother of invention.

All manner of swords, sabers, and bayonets are available from sutlers, as are firearms for reenacting. There is a very wide range of reproduction weapons available today. Infantry arms include the Model 1842 Springfield, Model 1855 Springfield, Model 1861 Springfield, and Model 1863 Springfield. Others, for Confederate use, include the Mississippi Rifle, Richmond Musket and Model 1853 Enfield. Sharps, Henry, and Spencer carbines are available for the cavalry trooper, along with the Colt Army, Colt Navy and Remington handguns. Remember to purchase a weapon that fits your impression. If you are creating the impression of an infantryman and are looking for a good basic weapon that would fit in almost anywhere, you cannot go wrong with a Model 1861 Springfield for a Union impression and a Model 1853 Enfield for a Confederate impression. Please remember that hand guns are for officers, cavalry and the occasional artilleryman, not for the basic infantryman. A pistol or a side knife stuck in a belt is only a safety risk and would not be allowed on the field on an infantryman at any respectable reenactment event.

An authentic reenactor does not only aspire to perfection of his impression on the field but also to the public in what the hobby calls "first person." The reenactor now becomes a living historian by taking on the identity of a War Between the States soldier. Create a person, know his life as you would your own, such as family, civilian job, etc. When in "first person" become that person, talk like him, act like him, and never stray from the 1860s as your time. As you become completely absorbed in the character the viewing public loves it and you both learn from it.

Carry only period items in your haversack and back pack. You should be able to open your haversack to the public and explain the contents. You should have items such as a sewing kit, pipe, twist of tobacco, straight razor, hard tack, coffee, harmonica, ambrotype or *cartes de visite* of the folks

Reenacting the War Between the States

BELOW: Canteens, one from tin, the other from wood. Today, as during the war, both could pose problems: the tin one will eventually impart a rust-colored tinge to the water, while the wooden one could spring a leak if the interior is not waxed.

BELOW RIGHT: This wounded Zouave wouldn't have worried about the color of the water in the canteen offered by his overcoat-clad foot soldier comrade. These men's clothes look somewhat ragged round the edges, and they probably feel the same way themselves. The reenactor's attire should look beaten up a bit too!

back home, tin plate, eating utensils and bible. These are just a few ideas, and such items can be found at the sutler or at your local antique mall.

Your campsite should also be where the public can view it and experience the 1860s. Nothing is worse for the hobby's reputation than to be walking through a camp and see a cooler or blow-up mattress. All cooking ware, tents, crates, bottles, rope, etc. should reflect the period. Should you wish to do a living history display at a National Park, State Park or museum contact them and send them a video of your living history camp and several "first person" presentations. Most of these types of organizations are unfamiliar with what you do and will want to see what you are all about before an invitation is extended. Never expect to do a battle reenactment or to fire your weapons at a living history event. All National Parks and some State Parks do not even allow you to bring black powder and caps onto their sites.

ABOVE: It's at the big reenactment events that the sounds, sights and smells of black powder discharges will be experienced, as in this Gettysburg event. Safety issues are uppermost in the minds of organizers and those responsible for the land and for the people in attendance.

Although the War Between the States was primarily an infantryman's war many reenactors today are drawn to join the cavalry or artillery units. The prohibitive cost of maintaining horses and saddlery, and the demanding training program to school a cavalryman and his horse, prevent all but a few living history groups from being mounted cavalry. The first major recreation of a cavalry action took place at Brandy Station, Virginia, in 1984 with about 200 mounted troopers. This was a major turning point for the mounted hobby, and it has spurred many outstanding mounted groups today.

The early reenactments of the 1960s saw mostly one-third and one-half scale cannon. Today, major events only allow full-size ordnance. Being an artillery reenactor is hard work. Most gun crews do not have horse-drawn limber and cannon, and must wheel their guns into action themselves. There are today a few fortunate groups that can afford the six-horse team and the training to master it. There are few sights to equal a horse-drawn gun team on the reenactment battlefield.

Today, War Between the States reenactors include those portraying not only soldiers but civilians, including servants, photographers, doctors, nurses and undertakers. At the reenactment of the Battle of Gettysburg in 1988 there was even a wagonload of "hookers," non-practicing of course. Several publications are available to keep up with the reenactment events, which constantly change: to be recommended are *Camp Chase Gazette* and *The Civil War News*. Civilian reenactors may find it useful to read *The Citizen's Companion*.

The hobby of War Between the States reenacting has come a great distance in its fifty-plus year history. For the Civil War buff it remains the ideal way to experience history at first hand, and just for that brief moment, you can really be there....

Uniforms Weapons and Equipment

By Russ A. Pritchard

ABOVE: Le Mat 2nd Model revolver, in .41/65 caliber. This weapon belonged to Captain J. N. Maffatt of the Confederate Navy, although the type was used by both sides during the war.

LEFT: Soldiers of the 22nd New York, dressed in a variety of general issue and non-regulation attire, pose outside their A-frame tent; this was designed to give shelter for four men, but more often than not would have to stretch to accommodate more.

Uniforms, Weapons and Equipment: Introduction

THE CIVIL WAR was the first modern war experienced by the American soldier. It occurred at a point in time when ordnance technology far out-paced medical science to the disastrous detriment of the participants. This was a war fought with modern weapons but obsolete tactics and the battlefield was the learning ground, the killing ground, for this hard lesson. Men on each side endured hardships during long weeks of campaigning and bitter winters in isolated, unsanitary camps the conditions of which we can only imagine. They faced a new and frightening killing machine in each battle – long range rifled small arms and artillery fire – and were still capable of incredible heroism in the face of almost certain death. The Union and Confederate soldiers set a standard for bravery and fortitude that has never been surpassed. In retrospect, we realize that there were no villains or despots as we saw in

FAR LEFT: Captain and private in the U.S. Artillery early in the war. Red is the artillery branch of service color, as shown in the officer's trouser stripe and shoulder strap, and the relevant insignia is crossed cannons, as shown on the private's kepi.

LEFT: Confederate officers of cavalry, infantry, and artillery. The cavalry major at left wears the so-called butternut-colored uniform that became common when dyes were too scarce to produce a uniform gray. Standing next to him is an infantry captain who also shows some ersatz in his dress. His uniform is proper gray, but his hat is definitely a makeshift substitution. Seated is a full colonel of artillery, and he at least has everything right. This was the rarity and probably indicates that he was uniformed early in the war.

the 20th century. Some of the prominent characters have achieved a larger than life stature in the years since the war and Generals Grant and Lee are universally known and admired. All the men were heroes. All the men were Americans.

Standardization, interchangeability and practicality are key principles that had a great impact during the war. In all previous wars on the American continent and overseas armies were dressed in bright, multicolored uniforms for the most part to facilitate identification of troops. Different regiments in the same army wore distinctive uniforms so that each could be identified, and the armies were much smaller. By the middle of the 19th century the Federal Army had dispensed with turn-back collars and contrasting facings, and had adopted a practical blue uniform and forage cap that looked good, was relatively inexpensive and easy to manufacture. Instead of different uniforms for different branches of service a major effort was made to standardize the uniform and utilize distinctive insignia. Union blue and Confederate gray became almost indistinguishable after a few days on the march and were the aegis of subdued uniforms of our modern armies. The green uniforms adopted by Berdan's Sharpshooters may be considered one of the forerunners of camouflage.

The rubberized ground cloth was a major advancement in personal comfort and shelter for the soldier. The Model 1858 canteen was the first mass-produced metal canteen in American service and remained the standard for half a century. The shelter half for the individual soldier was the forerunner of the pup tent known to so many 20th century soldiers. The stamped identification disks sold by sutlers to the soldiers were the beginning of dog tags that every soldier wears today, and corps badges developed into shoulder patches and DI's, distinctive insignia, as we know them.

The advances in ordnance were staggering. The Army had just adopted as standard a reduced bore, parts-interchangeable rifle-musket in 1855. It was further simplified with the production of the Model 1861 and over one million were produced during the war. This rifle-musket was accurate at 300 yards and replaced a smoothbore Model 1842 that was inaccurate at 100 yards. The Henry and Spencer rifles were the first magazine-fed, metallic-cartridge firearms used by the military. The Henry, the ancestor of the modern day Winchester rifle, fired a .44 caliber rimfire cartridge and was loaded with fifteen cartridges in a tube beneath the barrel. Actuation of the lever fed a round from the magazine into the chamber and also cocked the weapon. The Spencer fired a .52 caliber rimfire cartridge and was loaded with seven cartridges in an insertable tubular magazine in the buttstock. Actuation of the lever fed a round into the chamber but the weapon had to be cocked manually. Compared with the flintlock musket in production twenty years before, either arm was more than revolutionary. The revolver had been accepted grudgingly over the single-shot Model 1842 pistol and Colt and Remington handguns were obtained in large numbers. The metallic cartridge was perfected just before the war and numbers of breechloading carbines with patent mechanisms were in the trial stage. Weapons such as these sounded the death knell of the saber and sword that hereafter were

Uniforms, Weapons and Equipment: Introduction

demoted to the status of cumbersome badges of rank and relegated to baggage trains in many cases.

The Requa Battery Gun, the Ager Coffee Mill Gun, the Gatling Gun and the Vandenburgh Volley gun all were progenitors of the modern day machine gun. While not fully automatic, they were massed fire weapons and their effect, both physical and psychological, was not lost on the military minds of the day.

The Hanes, Ketchum and Raines patent hand grenades foretold of advances in defensive and offensive hand thrown weapons. Fuzes and fragmentation had not been perfected but their advantages in trench warfare were obvious.

Artillery had made great strides too. While smoothbore artillery was still in use and would remain so, rifled field artillery was being developed that greatly increased range and accuracy, with definite advantages. Fuzes for projectiles used in these guns were becoming more sophisticated. Timed fuzes facilitated air bursts and percussion fuzes allowed ground bursts. Segmented shell and the Mallet polygonal cavity projectile allowed more uniform fragmentation. Then there were the small Coehorn mortars, light enough to be carried by four men; these accompanied the infantry in the assault, giving them immediate and mobile artillery support. Hale's patent rocket launcher, though inaccurate, was another embryonic fire support system that developed into recoilless systems used in the 20th century. Small modified artillery rounds with special fuzes were the beginning of modern anti-personnel mines and land mine warfare.

Aerial observation became a reality with Lowe's observation balloon in 1862, and communication with flare pistols, wig wag flags and the telegraph greatly increased command and control on the battlefield.

The ironclad armored ship revolutionized the Navy. The days of iron men and wooden ships were past. John Ericsson's revolving turret on monitor-class ships foretold of the demise of sailing ships and broadsides. The development of armor-punching heavy projectiles to destroy armored ships followed quickly. Electrically detonated mines as we know them today were developed for naval use, and efforts were made to develop underwater craft, the ill-fated CSS Hunley becoming the first submersible to sink a ship with a torpedo.

BELOW: Longarm advances included breechloading repeating rifles, the Spencer below, introduced in 1863, and bottom the Henry, forerunner to the Winchester.

RIGHT: Revolvers, such as the Smith & Wesson No. 1 Second Issue right, as used by many Federal officers, and the Confederates' Leech and Rigdon bottom right began to replace the sword as a personal weapon.

The armies themselves had changed, too. In the 18th century armies were a few thousand, perhaps rising to ten thousand troops, whereas the Civil War witnessed the million-man army.

One has to observe all these incredible advances as if through the eyes of a naive young man who probably had never left his home town, certainly not the county. He was suddenly thrust into this huge army of strange men from all over the country, some speaking languages foreign to him, and exposed to all these new instruments of death and destruction. There is no question that all Civil War veterans remembered the war as the high point in their lives, a benchmark from which to judge all other experiences.

Some wag said that the Union Quartermaster Department and Ordnance facilities worked miracles. They managed to keep both Federal and Confederate armies armed and equipped in the field for four years. There is some truth in that. It is also obvious that without the nearly half a million longarms and tons of other material, military and civilian, that were run through the blockade from England the Confederacy could not have survived as long as she did. The glue that sustained the Union and Confederate forces through four long years of war has never ceased to be a topic of intense study. Since the Centennial, interest has continued to grow and now Hollywood has discovered the Civil War.

It is hoped that information and data in this volume will enable interested individuals to have a better understanding of the military material culture of the mid-19th century. We have attempted to put together a reference work for reenactors and living history activists who strive for authenticity of uniforms, weapons and equipment in all theaters, campaigns and battles as illustrated and represented by actual artifacts, artworks and period photographs reproduced in this volume. The efforts of reenactors and living history personnel are one avenue that will insure the memories of the heroes of 1861-1865 will be kept alive for future generations.

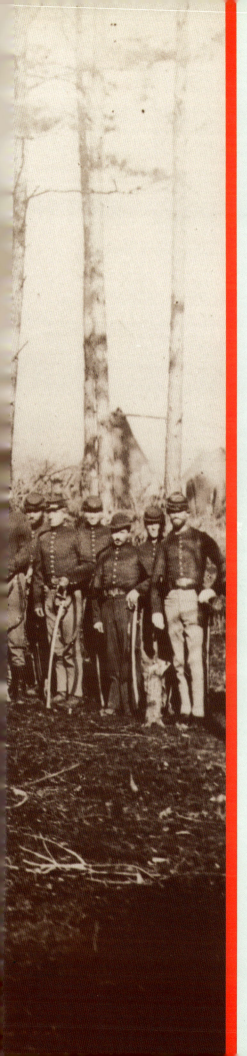

Equipment of the Federal Forces

ABOVE: Waist belt as issued to the Federal enlisted foot soldier during the period 1861-63.

LEFT: Photographed in February 1864, a detachment of the 1st U.S. Cavalry at Brandy Station, Va, where the North's horsemen came of age in the greatest cavalry battle of the war some eight months earlier.

OFFICERS' COATS AND JACKETS

FEDERAL OFFICERS' COATS and jackets were to be found in three basic styles: the frock, sack and shell. The frock coat generally followed the Uniform Regulations of 1851 and 1861 but non-regulation sack coats and shell jackets showed considerable latitude as officers purchased uniforms at their own expense. All were made of dark blue wool of varying quality and were lined with dark polished cotton or silk fabric. Rank and branch of service was designated by shoulder straps or epaulets bearing rank insignia on specific color backgrounds, single- or double-breasted construction, and button placement. Rank devices, buttons and branch of service colors will be discussed in detail in later sections.

The frock coat, which was very serviceable and probably the most frequently encountered, had a skirt extending from two-thirds to three-fourths of the distance from the top of the hip to the bend of the knee. There were generally two interior pockets within the lining of the rear of the skirt and a left-

General George G. Meade's uniform blouse, hat and cap, sword belt and sash, field glasses and case, presentation sword and two scabbards, and epaulets.

General William T. Sherman's uniform coat, with velvet collar and cuffs, and sash.

40   EQUIPMENT OF THE FEDERAL FORCES

hand breast pocket. The coat was double-breasted for general and field grade officers and single-breasted for company grade officers. General officers' coats usually had black velvet collars and cuffs. Staff officers' buttons for major generals and above were arranged in two rows of nine buttons in groups of three. Brigadier generals had two rows of eight buttons arranged in groups of two. Field grade officers have two rows of seven buttons each. All company grade officers had only one row of nine buttons. Field grade and company grade officers' buttons may have indicated branch of service.

The officers' sack coat appeared in double- and single-breasted configuration in various lengths from hip to thigh and with four to six buttons. Interior and exterior pockets have been noted. These coats were non-regulation and varied widely depending on the whim of the officer. Certain insignia, color of shoulder strap, and button type and placement were indicative of rank.

Front and rear views of Pennsylvania infantry officer's coat, with 5th Corps badge.

Engineer company grade officer's uniform coat, front and rear.

Officers' Coats and Jackets

The officers' shell jacket also appeared in both double- and single-breasted styles. Most were waist length but some have been noted slightly longer. Rank and branch of service were distinguished as noted above, although some of these jackets had additional galloons on the sleeves, while the number of strands also denoted rank. Some single-breasted jackets had nine to twelve buttons. These jackets seem to have been worn mostly by mounted officers of all branches and were authorized stable jackets for mounted artillery and cavalry.

Besides these three general styles in use with the bulk of the Army there were coats such as the pleated, pullover Rhode Island coat, the bottle-green frock coat of Berdan's Sharpshooters, and special Zouave shell jackets that were unit specific. Some of these will be discussed or illustrated in later sections.

Front and rear view of 6th Pennsylvania officer's jacket.

Short jacket of Lt. Col. William Fowler, 146th New York Regiment (Zouaves).

Captain Dillingham's Vermont Infantry sack coat, front and rear.

Officer's cloak coat.

OFFICERS' COATS AND JACKETS **43**

OFFICERS' TROUSERS

THE TWO BASIC types of officers' trousers were those for foot officers and those for mounted officers. According to General Order 108 dated December 16, 1861, trouser material was sky blue kersey for all regimental officers and the dark blue wool cloth as used for coats and jackets for all other officers. This change met mixed acceptance since dark blue trousers were in evidence throughout the war. Trousers had tin, bone or porcelain buttons for fly closure and suspenders on the waistband, a cotton waistband lining, adjustable belt rear vent closure and no rear pockets or loops for a waist belt.

Trousers for dismounted officers were usually not lined. There was a watch pocket in the waistband and two pockets, either side seam or mule ear, on the hip.

Trousers for mounted officers had a reinforced or double thickness seat and leg inseam, and there were sometimes foot straps at the cuff to hold the trouser leg down to the boot when mounted. Some mounted officers' trousers were also fully or partially lined with muslin or similar fabric and had the same pocket arrangement as dismounted men's trousers.

All trousers, with the exception of those of general officers, had a one-eighth inch staff or branch of service color welt let into the outside seam of both legs. Specific colors will be discussed in a later section.

Besides the two general styles there were also trousers for officers of distinctive organizations such as Zouaves and some state units that varied in color and cut.

BELOW: No special trousers were issued for this special officer! Lieutenant General Ulysses S. Grant was unconcerned and unconventional concerning the matter of dress and rank insignia: here he's wearing a coat with the three-button pattern of a major general over his unlined trousers which, correctly, show no branch of service welt.

General and staff officers' trousers, front and rear.

44 EQUIPMENT OF THE FEDERAL FORCES

Cavalry officer's trousers, front and rear.

Infantry officer's trousers, front and rear.

ENLISTED MEN'S TROUSERS 45

Officers' Hats and Caps

THE MOST PROMINENT styles of Federal Officers' headgear were the Forage Cap, the Pattern 1858 Officers' Hat and the Slouch Hat. These hats were found in numerous configurations and many were further altered to the individual preference.

Besides the then current patterns there were some obsolete hats and shakos still in use with state and militia units and there were a small number of patent types in limited use. One season of hard campaigning insured the survival of only the most practical equipment.

The familiar Civil War pattern Forage Cap was authorized in 1858 to replace the Pattern 1839. Today, this type of hat is universally called the Kepi, from the French 'Kappe'. The cap was made of blue wool cloth with a leather chin strap attached by brass buttons and a leather visor. It had a silk or polished cotton lining, sometimes with the manufacturer or retailers' name in gilt letters marked in the crown, and had a wide thin leather sweatband. Two styles were quite popular and named after the respective Generals who wore them. The McDowell style had a high floppy crown and rounded, sharply slopping visor. The McClellan or Chasseur Style had a much lower crown and squared, slightly angled visor. War Department General Order No. 6 dated March 13, 1861 stated that all officers

Slouch hat worn by Major General George G. Meade at Gettysburg.

Meade's forage cap, worn during 1864 campaigns.

46 EQUIPMENT OF THE FEDERAL FORCES

Model 1859 chapeau.

Major General John Sedgwick's slouch hat.

McDowell pattern forage cap.

Light artillery shako

OFFICERS' HATS AND CAPS 47

Officers' Hats and Caps

would wear respective branch insignia on the front of the Forage Cap. Unit numerals and various corps badges were also worn at the discretion of the officer. These insignia and badges are discussed in detail in a later section.

The Forage Cap worn by Zouave and some Chasseur officers was the same configuration but surviving specimens were made of red wool with gold lace quatrefoil on the top and gold lace stripes around the hat band that are rank indicative following the French style.

Another popular more formal hat was the Pattern 1858 Officers' Hat. Today, it is called the Hardee Hat honoring William J. Hardee who sat on the officers' board that adopted it. The same hat is also referred to as the Jeff Davis Hat because Mr. Davis was Secretary of War when it was adopted.

Slouch hat of Lt. Henry M Brewster, 57th New York Infantry, with badge of 2nd Corps, 1st Division.

Staff officer's forage cap worn by Capt. Charles P. Pierce, on the staff of Brig. Gen. Henry M. Judah.

Chasseur's pattern cap with regimental insignia, actually that of Capt. Selleck L. White, 10th Connecticut Infantry.

Officer's slouch hat worn by First Lt. John A. Beall, 94th Ohio Infantry.

Patent havelock cap or "whipple hat," with battery insignia, as worn by Lt. George W. Taylor, 4th Massachusetts Battery. The unit name is stencilled in black on the front of the hat.

Standard infantry officer's McDowell-pattern forage cap with infantry insignia.

Forage cap with 10th Corps insignia, worn by Maj. Samuel S. Linton.

OFFICERS' HATS AND CAPS   49

Officers' Hats and Caps

This black, stiff fur felt hat was developed from the hat that was proscribed for cavalry officers that year and replaced the Pattern 1851 Hat for all Officers. The hat was usually lined with silk or other fine fabric and had a wide thin leather sweatband. The manufacturer or retailers' name was often embossed in gilt letters in the crown. It had a broad brim with the edge trimmed with black tape turned up on the right side and held in place by an embroidered eagle badge. Two black ostrich feathers on the left side indicated a company grade officer and three a field grade officer. The body of the hat was encircled by an officers' hat cord and the front of the hat bore branch and unit designation. All these insignia are discussed in a later section.

The Slouch Hat was a non-regulation soft crowned, broad brimmed dark brown or black felt hat of practical design and universal appeal. Most were lined similarly to the Pattern 1858 Officers'

Forage infantry cap of Captain Charles Burton.

Chasseur's pattern cap with regimental insignia, worn by First Lt. Peter Palen, 143rd New York Infantry.

Forage cap with regimental insignia, and patent air vent in the crown. It belonged to Capt. Lindley M. Coleman, 19th Maine Infantry.

Hat. This style was most popular with officers in the Western Theater but saw considerable service in the East. Many were privately purchased civilian hats with officers' hat cords, corps badges and branch insignia attached per regulations. There was enormous variety shade, size and shape based solely on the preference of the wearer.

Yet another style of hat was the hybrid Pattern 1858 Slouch Hat. The fine felt body had the softness of the slouch hat and the crown was often creased. Hat cord, insignia and ostrich plumes were worn per regulations. General Ambrose P. Burnside wore this style hat and it is referred to as the Burnside Hat.

The Chapeau Bras or French chapeau, Pattern 1840, had been discontinued with the uniform changes of 1851. War Department General Order No. 3 dated May 24, 1858 reauthorized this type

Forage cap of Lt. Col. William Fowler, 146th New York Regiment (Zouaves).

Forage cap of aide-de-camp W. H. Mallory, 5th New York Regiment (known as Duryee's Zouaves).

Forage cap of Maj. Gen. Gouverneur K. Warren, Meade's Chief Engineer, who also went on to command Meade's old V Corps at the Wilderness.

OFFICERS' HATS AND CAPS 51

Officers' Hats and Caps

of hat as optional for Field Grade and General Officers in lieu of the Pattern 1858 Officers' Hat. This fore and aft hat was relegated to dress uniform in garrison and saw no field use. It was made of beaver with the right side adorned with an intricate rosette of gold lace overlaid with a large silver or gilt eagle. The top of the hat was crowned with ostrich feathers, a magnificent but fragile piece.

There was one hat that was branch specific, the Light Artillery Officers' Cap. This hat was reauthorized in 1859 and was sometimes called the Ringgold Hat after the officer who made this style popular during the Mexican War. The hat has a stiff dark blue body with wide square leather visor, red horsehair plume above embroidered branch insignia and gilt cords and lines that drape the shoulder and breast of the uniform coat.

Forage cap of Second Lt. George W. Webb, Battery F, Independent Pennsylvania Artillery; here crossed cannon are on a badge.

Artillery officer's forage cap worn by Capt. J. Henry Sleeper, 10th Massachusetts Battery.

Cavalry officer's forage cap, with crossed-sabers insignia, which could have been embroidered or in stamped metal.

EQUIPMENT OF THE FEDERAL FORCES

Slouch hat of Second Ltd. Levi J. Homan, Ementrout's Independent Company of Pennsylvania Artillery.

Cavalry officer's slough hat worn by Capt. Alexander H. McHenry, Co. G, 13th Pennsylvania Cavalry.

Cavalry officer's slough hat of the 4th U.S. Cavalry.

Officer's cap of 114th Pennsylvania Volunteer Infantry, Collis' Zouaves (many of whose enlisted men began the war wearing turbans).

OFFICERS' HATS AND CAPS 53

ENLISTED MEN'S COATS AND JACKETS

FEDERAL ENLISTED MEN'S COATS and jackets can be found in the same basic styles as officers': the frock coat, sack coat, and shell jacket. The garments were usually of lesser quality, manufactured at arsenals and by numerous contractors. Many early coats were said to be made of "shoddy," a kind of remanufactured material. Some of these coats were so poor that they literally fell apart or dissolved in the rain. This was the result of manufacturers' profiteering, which was soon corrected by a system of Quartermaster Inspectors. As the war continued it became evident that efforts were being made to establish a standard of dress for the whole Army.

The 1858 Regulations authorized and required a single-breasted dark blue frock coat with nine brass buttons for all enlisted soldiers. The 1861 Regulations stated that the skirt extended one-half the distance from the top of the hip to the bend of the knee and the stand-up collar was hooked at the neck. Brass scale epaulets were worn on the shoulders for dress functions. There were pockets in the rear skirt of the coat and one in the breast. Lining was usually polished cotton. Many coats were government issued but there were some that were privately purchased by those who could afford them, and these were found to be of officer quality in some cases. The collar and cuffs with two brass

Front and rear views of infantryman's frock coat.   Front and rear views of artilleryman's frock coat.

Engineer 1st sergeant's frock coat.

Artilleryman's jacket, front and rear.

Cavalry musician's jacket, front and rear.

ENLISTED MEN'S COATS AND JACKETS 55

Enlisted Men's Coats and Jackets

Veteran Reserve Corps jacket, front and rear.

Four-buttoned sack coat, front and rear.

Four-buttoned sack coat of 1st sergeant of Artillery.

State issue infantry jacket of 1863, of the New York State Militia and National Guard.

Shell jacket of sergeant, 6th Pennsylvania Cavalry ("Rush's Lancers").

buttons were piped with cord or welt in branch of service color. These colors will be discussed in a later section. These frock coats were relegated to garrison duty by many units but some regiments, such as those in the Iron Brigade, proudly wore their long coats in the field.

The dark blue sack coat was the trademark of Billy Yank. It was adopted for fatigue duties in 1859 and became the uniform of choice of the Union Army by late 1861. Tens of thousands were manufactured during the war at Schuylkill Arsenal in Philadelphia, Cincinnati Arsenal, and a host of private and commercial contractors. The coat was made of loose fitting dark blue flannel extending half way down the thigh. It was single-breasted with four brass buttons and an interior breast pocket, and came in lined and unlined styles. The sack coat was easy to manufacture, inexpensive and practical, an ideal military garment. Because of these factors, most were worn-out in service, and it is a rare coat today.

Artillery and cavalry shell jackets were of the same pattern. The 1861 Regulations stated that they would be made of dark blue cloth with one row of twelve small brass buttons and a stiff stand-up

Unique shell jacket of 3rd New Jersey Cavalry (the "Butterflies").

Distinctive shell jacket of sergeant, 11th New York Cavalry ("Scott's 900").

ENLISTED MEN'S COATS AND JACKETS 57

Enlisted Men's Coats and Jackets

collar hooked at the neck. Brass scale epaulets were worn on the shoulders for dress functions but were not worn in the field. The jacket extended to the waist and the collar, cuffs and all edges were piped with three-eighths-inch wide tape in the color of branch of service. The jacket was supposed to be lined with white flannel but a variety of colored fabrics have been observed too. Many volunteer artillery and cavalry units came into service with their own state issue of these regulation patterns, and these exhibit many subtle variations. There existed some very few dragoon and mounted rifle shell jackets in the early months of the war. These were according to pattern with lace in color of branch of service. Musicians of these branches wore the same shell jacket with the addition of an elaborate pattern of tape in the form of a plastron on the breast.

New York State 1861 issue shell jackets were another variation of this pattern. These jackets had cloth epaulets and a belt loop on the left side. The epaulets, belt loop and sometimes the collar were piped in branch of service color.

1861 New York State jacket, with rear view at top right.

1863 New York National Guard jacket, with rear view at left.

58 EQUIPMENT OF THE FEDERAL FORCES

Typical field gear for a Federal sergeant, including belt with bayonet in scabbard, pouch for percussion caps, a shoulder belt, canteen, knapsack, and haversack.

Front and rear views of jacket and vest of sergeant, Birrey's Zouaves, 23rd Pennsylvania Infantry.

ENLISTED MEN'S COATS AND JACKETS 59

ENLISTED MEN'S COATS AND JACKETS

Zouave shell jackets were all based on the jacket worn by the elite French North African units. Almost all had the decorative device known as tombeaux on each breast and the collarless, short, close fitting jacket did not button but had an integral vest worn beneath the coat. The tombeaux were normally bright red on the dark blue jacket. These jackets, along with other striking pieces of Zouave uniform, made the soldier so attired a handsome target.

Somewhat less conspicuous were the chasseur coats, copies from those of the French Light Infantry. These were worn by some Pennsylvania, New York, and Massachusetts units and were made of dark blue cloth, slightly flared and longer than a shell jacket but not as long or shapeless as the sack coat. Lining was dark polished cotton and similar fabric. Most had epaulets, belt loops, and colored piping, and some were actually imported from France.

On all of these uniforms chevrons in branch of service color above the elbow indicated noncommissioned officer rank.

Jacket of sergeant, 6th Pennsylvania Cavalry, with rear view at top right.

Jacket worn by enlisted man, Anderson Cavalry (Pennsylvania), with rear view at left.

Front and rear views of 9th New York Infantry (Hawkins' Zouaves) jacket and vest.

Front and rear views of 95th Pennsylvania Infantry (Gosline Zouaves) jacket and vest.

Overcoat for enlisted foot soldier, front and rear.

Overcoat for enlisted mounted man, front and rear.

ENLISTED MEN'S COATS AND JACKETS 61

ENLISTED MEN'S TROUSERS

TROUSERS FOR ENLISTED men, like those of officers, were found in mounted and dismounted patterns. All trousers were made to be loose fitting with the cuff spread well over the boot. The seat and inside of the trouser leg were reinforced for mounted personnel. The 1861 Regulations ordered all trousers to be dark blue cloth with the exception of Light Artillery units, whose trousers were to be sky blue kersey. General Order No. 108, Headquarters of the Army, dated December 16, 1861, said every enlisted man except those of the Ordnance Branch would wear sky blue kersey trousers. Ordnance personnel retained the dark blue trousers.

Trousers for foot soldiers were usually not lined and had metal, bone or porcelain buttons for fly closure and suspenders. Pockets were either side seam or mule ear and there were never any rear pockets or belt loops.

Noncommissioned officers had worsted leg stripes in branch of service color. Sergeant's stripes were one-and-one-half inches wide and those for a corporal were a half-inch wide.

Some Zouave trousers were, in fact, pantaloons in the style borrowed from the North African dress of the crack French Zouave units. The leg came only below the knee and was bloused in the gaiters or jambiéres worn with this uniform. Many of the pants were cut very full. Others were tailored more like conventional trousers but each regiment had its own distinctive style. Some of the pantaloons were bright red, others shades of blue. Combined with other pieces of the uniform, these made the Zouaves very conspicuous on the battlefield.

Trousers of enlisted foot soldier (private), front and rear.   Cavalry corporal's trousers, front and rear.

62 EQUIPMENT OF THE FEDERAL FORCES

Engineer sergeant's trousers, front (above) and rear (below).

Trousers of Hawkins' Zouaves (9th New York Infantry, front (above) and rear (below).

Trousers of 1st sergeant, Birrey's Zouaves (23rd Pennsylvania Infantry), front (above) and rear (below).

ENLISTED MEN'S TROUSERS 63

ENLISTED MEN'S SHIRTS, AND NECK SOCKS

SHIRTS FOR THE soldier were always a pullover pattern, often of coarse wool material or sometimes flannel, and cut very full. Colors varied from shades of white and gray to dark blue and many civilian shirts of plaid and striped patterns were worn when issue items were not available. They were considered undergarments and rarely worn without the coat. Most had two to four bone buttons at the neck and one bone button on each cuff. There were no pockets in military contract shirts but many civilian shirts had one or two.

Like the sack coat, shirts were worn-out in service and are seldom seen today. Three shirts a year were supposedly issued to each enlisted man. Prolonged periods in the field made this very difficult to

Blue flannel shirt, front and rear.

White linen shirt.

BELOW: Enlisted men wore their shirts until they practically fell off their backs. When lounging around camp they would often grab the chance to shuck their uniform jackets or coats, like the soldier at right, although shirts were regarded as undergarments and thus seldom seen without a coat.

accomplish. These garments were secured from a multitude of contractors and surviving specimens are very diverse. Several states also issued shirts to their regiments and they, too, show considerable individuality.

The 1851 and 1861 Regulations specified all enlisted men were to have a leather neck stock "of the pattern then in use." It was thought that such an item would keep the soldier's head up and give him a more martial bearing. It was little more than a band of leather with a small buckle worn under the collar, very uncomfortable in practice. Most were left in garrison or thrown away in the field at the first opportunity.

Enlisted man's necksock.

Officer's necksock.

ENLISTED MEN'S SHIRTS, AND NECK SOCKS 65

Enlisted Men's Hats and Caps

The 1858 Pattern enlisted men's hat, known as the Hardee hat, was made of black felt and had a double row of stitching instead of binding around the edge. The brim was looped up on the right for mounted men and on the left for foot soldiers, and a black feather was worn on the side opposite the loop. The hat had a worsted branch of service color hat cord with tassels and branch of service insignia on the front. All insignia, unit numeral, branch of service plate and eagle plate, were made of die stamped brass. Many Hardee hats were field-modified by soldiers to be almost unrecognizable.

The enlisted Pattern 1861 forage cap was the hat worn by most Federal soldiers throughout the war. Civilian contractors sold over four million of them to the Quartermaster Department and

Light Artillery shako, with stamped metal insignia.

M1858 forage cap.

M1858 uniform (Hardee) hat for infantryman, brim down.

M1858 uniform (Hardee) hat for artilleryman.

M1858 uniform (Hardee) hat for engineer.

M1858 uniform (Hardee) hat for infantryman, brim up.

ENLISTED MEN'S HATS AND CAPS

Enlisted Men's Hats and Caps

another 41,000 were manufactured at Army Depots. Enlisted men also wore chasseur pattern forage caps with a lower crown. Branch of service insignia, company letter, and regimental numerical designation and corps badge were on the top of these hats rather than the front. With the exception of the corps badge, all insignia was die stamped brass.

Early in the conflict forage and chasseur pattern caps were often covered by havelocks made of cotton or linen. These covers supposedly provided protection from sun and dust on the march but actually added to the discomfort of the wearer. Most were discarded or the material put to some other

Hardee hat, with artillery branch color (red) very prominent.

Hardee hat with plume, worn by First Sergeant Harlan Cobb, Engineers.

Zouave fez worn by Cpl. Walter H. Mallorie, Co. B, 76th Pennsylvania Volunteers ("Keystone" Zouaves")

Fez, with regimental badge, owned by Pte. Latham Avery Fish, Co. C, 9th New York Volunteer Infantry, and worn at Antietam.

Forage cap worn by gunners.

Forage cap worn by cavalrymen.

Shako of 7th New York Regiment, New York National Guard, with plate, chin strap, and cockade.

Model 1851 Albert style hat of the 50th Regiment, New York National Guard.

ENLISTED MEN'S HATS AND CAPS

Enlisted Men's Hats and Caps

use. Waterproof or foul weather covers made of oilcloth or vulcanized rubber were used and welcomed by sentries and videtes during inclement weather.

Civilian slouch hats were very popular particularly with Western Theater troops. These hats were usually dark, nondescript and shaped to the whim of the soldier. Some had appropriate regulation military insignia affixed.

Zouave units affecting the uniform of French colonial troops wore a wool fez, usually red, and sometimes a white turban. Other special units wore specific headgear such as the bottle green forage caps of Berdan's Sharpshooters and the French Pattern shako of the 83rd Pennsylvania Volunteer Infantry. A few militia leather shakos were seen early in the war before Federal troops were issued regular uniforms.

Illinois Volunteers Hardee hat.

Fez worn by Private Thaddeus Paxon, Co. F, 114th Pennsylvania Volunteers ("Collis' Zouaves").

Patent rubber rain hat.

70 EQUIPMENT OF THE FEDERAL FORCES

NGSNY chasseur cap.

Zouave fez.

7th New York State Militia shako.

M1858 regulation shako of 50th New York State Militia.

ENLISTED MEN'S HATS AND CAPS

Footwear

The Pattern 1851 Jefferson Brogan was the standard army shoe. It was called a bootee and was made of tanned leather with the rough side out. It had a high top over the ankle, laced with four eyelets and had a squared toe. Sizes were from 5 to 12. Most had metal plates attached to toe and heel to extend serviceability of the shoe. Regulations required brogans to be blackened. Bootblack was available from the unit sutler. The Quartermaster Department was the source of this equipment until the huge expansion of the Army brought on by the war. At that time the government was forced to resort to contracts with civilian supply sources, with initially mixed results.

Some early reports stated that brogans lasted less than two weeks because of poor material and fabrication. Some were even said to have lasted only hours. Fortuitously, the prewar shoe industry was

Enlisted men's style of boots (although this pair were worn by an officer).

Officers' boots, with spurs.

Standard booties.

72   EQUIPMENT OF THE FEDERAL FORCES

well established in Northern states and war profiteering was brought under control. Eventually an adequate supply of quality footwear became available although there were periodic shortages.

A surprising number of shoes were imported from England and fine English brogans captured from blockade-runners and from Confederate soldiers have been noted. There were also a limited number of canvas-topped civilian camp or leisure-time shoes that were utilized

Mounted personnel usually wore high leather boots. Enlisted men were issued boots but officers' boots were usually acquired by private purchase. Officers' boots were very diverse. Some were dragoon style that came over the mid-thigh, others over the knee, and some just to the top of the calf.

Zouave jambieres or outer leggings (greaves).

Zouave jambieres, plus gaiters, worn by Cpl. Walter H. Mallorie, Co. B, 76th Pennsylvania Volunteers ("Keystone Zouaves").

Federal-issue leggings.

Leather boots of Major General George G. Meade.

Cavalry officer's high boots.

Branch and Unit Insignia and Decorations of Officers

Officers' branch of service insignia was of higher quality than that of enlisted personnel, although they wore the same devices, such as the curled horn for infantry. Artillery wore crossed cannon; cavalry, crossed sabers; engineers, a castle; ordnance, a bomb. The device was made of gold thread embroidered on a black velvet ground attached to headgear, as per 1851/1861 regulations. Unit insignia began as a piece of colored cloth affixed to the top of the forage cap so that officers could identify personnel of a particular division. Different heraldic designs such as the circle, star, shield and diamond, were assigned to corps, and different colors were assigned to divisions within the corps. Red was first division, blue second and white third.

No decorations for valor or service existed at the beginning of the war. The Medal of Honor was authorized by Congress in 1862 and was the first such award.

Special medals such as the Kearny Medal were fabricated in extremely limited numbers and worn by officers who served in the 1st Division, 3rd Corps, before November 1862.

Pattern 1851 infantry officer's stamped brass insignia.

Cavalry officer's stamped brass insignia.

Pattern 1851 artillery officer's stamped brass insignia.

Embroidered regimental insignia for officer's Hardee hat: Captain Langhorne Wister, 13th Regiment, Pennsylvania Reserves.

Pattern 1851 cavalry officer's embroidered hat insignia.

Pattern 1851 officer's embroidered eagle (all service insignia).

Rifle officer's Hardee hat insignia of the 8th New York Regiment (German Rifles).

Rifle officer's hat insignia.

Artillery officer's insignia: Lt. G. W. Taylor, 4th MA Battery.

Hat insignia of Colonel Augustus Funk, 39th New York (also known as the Garibaldi Guard).

BRANCH AND UNIT INSIGNIA AND DECORATIONS OF OFFICERS

Branch and Unit Insignia and Decorations of Enlisted men

ENLISTED MEN'S INSIGNIA was fabricated from die stamped sheet brass. Artillery, cavalry, engineers, and ordnance symbols were the same as for officers. The steel dies for many of these insignia still exist and re-stamps from original dies were plentiful through the 1960s.

Unit insignia, including heraldic designs and colors for corps and divisions, were similar to those for officers. Enlisted men's badges were field-fabricated from bone or cloth or purchased from a sutler in precious metal. The use of the corps badge became increasingly popular and it was not unusual to find the badge field-applied to canteen and haversack, and even carved in the stock of a longarm. The division and corps flags all adopted these symbols, all of such heraldry encouraging and highlighting the men's sense of comradeship and pride in their unit.

The Medal of Honor, awarded for conspicuous gallantry in battle, was authorized by Congress in 1862 and was the first real award for valor. More than 2,100 were awarded to soldiers, mostly enlisted men. Special medals, such as the Kearny Cross and the Gilmore Medal were fabricated in extremely limited numbers and worn by men who served in a particular unit or were in a particular engagement.

RIGHT: Crossed sabers on the hat clearly identify this enlisted man as cavalry. In fact he's a member of Co. E, 6th Pennsylvania Cavalry, "Rush's Lancers."

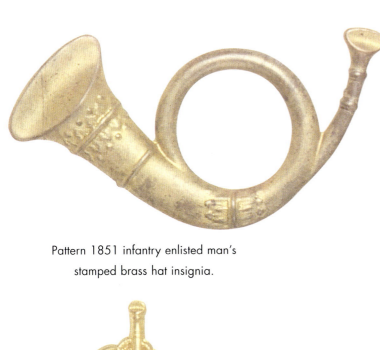

Pattern 1851 infantry enlisted man's stamped brass hat insignia.

Pattern 1851 engineer enlisted man's stamped brass insignia.

Pattern 1851 hat insignia for regiment of mounted riflemen.

Pattern 1858 hat insignia for regiment of mounted riflemen.

Pattern 1851 ordnance enlisted man's stamped brass insignia.

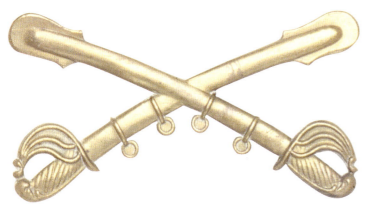

Pattern 1851 cavalry enlisted man's stamped brass insignia.

Pattern 1851 artillery enlisted man's stamped brass insignia.

BRANCH AND UNIT INSIGNIA AND DECORATIONS OF ENLISTED MEN

Insignia of Rank, Officer and Enlisted

Officer rank was primarily indicated by shoulder straps worn on the coat. Straps had a gilt border surrounding a field of velvet in branch of service color on which the rank was affixed. Straps were usually sewn to the coat but some had strings or ribbons that attached through eyelets in the fabric of the coat. More expensive straps had several rows of gilt cord around the edge, and Smith's Patent straps had die stamped brass edges of simulated embroidery with brass insignia. As the war continued and officer casualties mounted, wearing of the insignia became more discreet; small insignia only were found on the collar, or on the shoulder without straps; or a single rank insignia may even have been

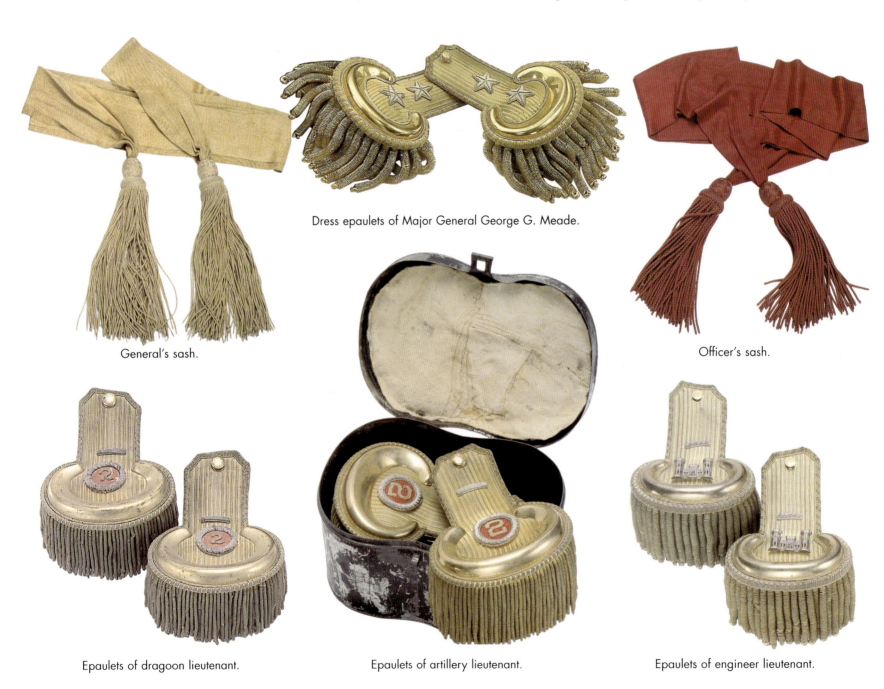

General's sash.

Dress epaulets of Major General George G. Meade.

Officer's sash.

Epaulets of dragoon lieutenant.

Epaulets of artillery lieutenant.

Epaulets of engineer lieutenant.

Infantry colonel's shoulder straps.

Cavalry lieutenant's shoulder straps.

Major general's shoulder straps.

Shoulder straps of 2nd lieutenant, artillery.

Epaulets of infantry lieutenant.

Brigadier general's shoulder straps.

Shoulder straps of 2nd lieutenant, infantry.

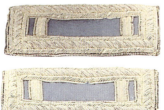

Shoulder straps of 1st lieutenant, infantry.

Staff captain's shoulder straps.

Lieutenant colonel's shoulder straps.

Colonel's shoulder straps.

INSIGNIA OF RANK, OFFICER AND ENLISTED

Insignia of Rank, Officer and Enlisted

pinned on the breast. Some officers' coats had gold cord gallons on the lower sleeve. Normally, this rank device was found on overcoats. The number of threads indicated rank: lieutenants had one, generals had six. Gilt and black tape quatrefoil on the top of a forage cap was also indicative of officer rank in the same manner as sleeve gallons. Dress epaulets were worn for parades and formal functions. They were large gilt thread shoulder boards with gilt fringe, and with rank insignia affixed to the board. The size of the gilt fringe also indicated rank.

Inverted vee sleeve chevrons in branch of service color indicated enlisted rank.

NCOs also wore a maroon or dark red worsted wool sword belt sash. Polished brass scale epaulets were worn on the shoulders for dress parade and formal events.

Shoulder straps of Captain Josiah Meigs, 2nd U.S. Colored Artillery.

Cavalry major's shoulder straps.

Cavalry captain's shoulder straps.

Noncommissioned officer's sash.

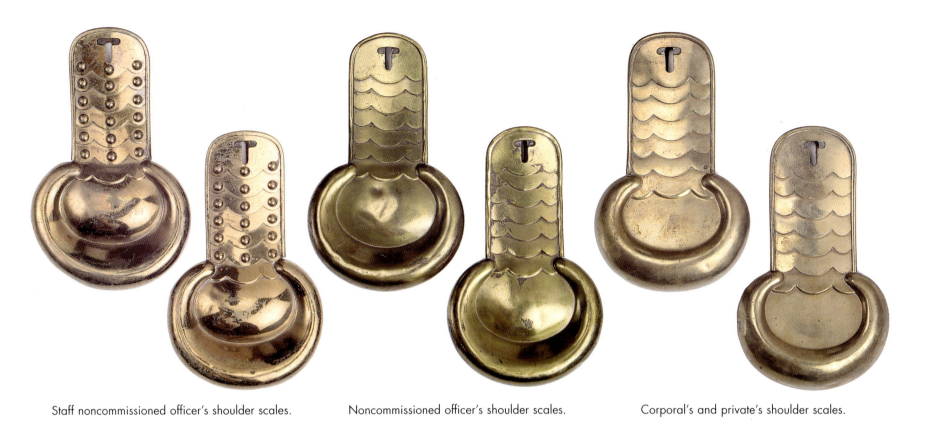

Staff noncommissioned officer's shoulder scales. Noncommissioned officer's shoulder scales. Corporal's and private's shoulder scales.

Second Lieutenant

Major

Brigadier General

First Lieutenant

Lieutenant Colonel

Major General

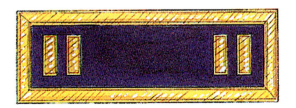

Captain

Colonel

Lieutenant General/General-in-Chief

INSIGNIA OF RANK, OFFICER AND ENLISTED

Corps Badges

CORPS BADGES WERE INSTITUTED in the Federal Army by a Circular dated March 21, 1863, signed by Major General Joseph Hooker. The stated purpose was to facilitate the ready identification of units and to prevent any injustice to units accused of poor conduct. Specific shapes were assigned to each corps and specific colors, red, white and blue, for each division within that corps. The first corps badges were cut from cloth and attached to the crown of the forage cap. Officers tended to have finer embroidered corps badges that were privately purchased.

The practice became very popular with the Army, and pin back metal badges became available for officers and enlisted men. These badges were usually worn on the breast of the uniform coat and they varied widely in quality. Some were available from local sutlers, made of white metal or stamped brass. A few have been noted carved from bone and tinted by individual soldiers. At the other end of the spectrum were those fabricated by jewelers in silver and gold with applied enamel colors and engraved with the owner's name and unit designation. Some even had battle honors inscribed on them. These corps badges were greatly prized and some were truly works of the jeweler's art. They are considered the forerunner of the modern Army unit shoulder patch, an important step in military heraldry.

Corps badge applied to top of forage cap worn by Colonel Charles P. Herring, 118th Pennsylvania Infantry.

1st Division, Fourth Corps badge.

Identification badge of Colonel Charles P. Herring, 118th Pennsylvania Infantry.

1st Division, Sixth Corps badge.

20th Corps badge of Lieutenant Samuel Goodman.

Identification badge of Lt. J. A. Rothermel, 19th Pennsylvania Cavalry.

1st Division, Fifth Corps pin of Captain N. Bayne.

1st Division, Sixth Corps badge of Brevet Major James W. Latta.

2nd Division, Third Corps badge.

Identification badge of Colonel P. J. Yorke, Bayards Brigade, 1st Pennnsylvania Cavalry.

3rd Division, Ninth Corps badge of Lieutenant William Goodrich.

Sheridan's Cavalry Corps Badge of Major John Cassals.

Fifth Corps badge of Brevet Brigadier General Charles P. Herring.

Colonel P. J. Yorke's Fifth Corps badge.

CORPS BADGES 83

Federal Buttons

FEDERAL BUTTONS WERE either die struck or cast. By far the most common method was the struck button, which was more durable than the cast variety, and the material of choice by the mid-19th century was thin rolled sheet brass. Buttons were decorative as well as functional and most exhibited some form of military heraldry on the face. Officers' buttons were generally decorated with national eagles or state seals. In some cases buttons were branch of service indicative. A button with an eagle surmounted by a shield bearing the raised letter I, C or A identified the wearer as an infantry officer, cavalry officer or artillery officer, respectively. Other branches of service such as engineers had a distinctive device on the button. The most common buttons were those worn by staff officers, the

Staff officer's button.

Staff officer's button.

Artillery officer's button.

Cavalry officer's button.

Dragoon officer's button.

Infantry officer's button.

Rifle officer's button.

Voltigeur officer's button.

Enlisted man's button.

Staff officer's button.

84 · EQUIPMENT OF THE FEDERAL FORCES

three branches of service already mentioned and all the state seal buttons. These buttons are found in three sizes usually: coat, cuff and vest.

Most buttons were known as three-piece buttons and had a face, back and shank. Many of the backs were struck with the name of the maker, and this was known as a backmark. The great majority of buttons had a gilt finish although some specialized few are found silvered.

The variety of buttons is very great. Die variations, sizes, and backmarks make this military object a very popular collecting specialty and large numbers have survived. As recent as the 1960s some Civil War buttons were still available on original cards just as they came from the factory.

Engineer officer's button.

Engineer officer's button.

Topographical engineer's button.

Ordnance button.

Ordnance button.

Goodyear's patent infantry button.

Variation of Goodyear button.

Variation of Goodyear button.

Massachusetts militia button.

New Hampshire militia button.

FEDERAL BUTTONS

Officers' Waist Belts

The standard waist belt for officers during the Civil War was the Pattern 1851 sword belt with rectangular brass sword belt plate. The individual officer privately purchased almost all sword belts and there was a wide range of quality. Sword belts were available from military regalia retailers such as Ball, Black & Co., Schuyler, Hartley & Graham, and Tiffany & Co. in New York City; Bailey & Co., Evans & Hassall, and W. H. Horstmann & Sons in Philadelphia; and M. W. Galt & Brothers and Hunt and Goodwin in Washington, D.C.

The 1851 and 1861 Regulations stated that the belt was to be not less than one-and-one-half inches wide nor more than two inches, and that the sword was to be suspended from two slings of the same material. The sword belt for General Officers was made of Russian leather with three gold bullion stripes on the belt and slings. The sword belt for all other officers was made of black leather.

Sword belts for all officers were normally plain black leather. Some have been noted with embossed lines only on the top and bottom edges, while others have been completely covered with embossed designs, and a few have been piped in branch of service color on the edges. The more elaborate belts were originally cased integral with high grade edged weapons. Earlier pattern sword belts and non-regulation types have been seen in contemporary photography but they are the exception to the rule.

The belt plate was rectangular in shape, made of cast brass and with a gilt finish. Some are found with an applied silver wreath. A small number have been noted with a fine chased finish and may have been made by a jeweler.

Rifle officer's sword belt.

M1851 general officer's "Russian" leather sword belt.

M1851 mounted (cavalry) sword belt.

M1855 rifle belt for saber bayonet.

Enlisted Men's Waist Belts

The 1851 Regulation black buff or black bridle leather waist belt with 1839 Pattern oval brass U.S. belt plate was the standard waist belt of the war. The belt was 1½ inches wide and 38½ inches long. A wide variety of waist belts used by the uniformed militias of the various states included some earlier obsolete patterns.

The 1851 Regulation dragoon and cavalry waist belts were black buff and later bridle leather. These belts were 1⅞ inches wide, had saber straps 1¹⁄₁₆ inches wide and over-the-shoulder straps 1⅛ inches wide. The Pattern 1851 rectangular sword belt plate was attached to the belt. A very similar belt without shoulder strap was issued for mounted light artillery personnel. Black buff and bridle leather belts with a frog to hold the Model 1832 foot artillery short sword were issued to NCOs officers of foot artillery units. This belt utilized the Pattern 1851 rectangular eagle plate.

The lead filled brass plate was 2½ x 3½ inches. The plate was attached to the belt by oval studs until 1863, when brass arrowhead hooks became standard. This belt supported the cap box and bayonet scabbard, and sometimes the cartridge box. The same black buff or bridle leather belt appeared fitted with the rectangular sword belt plate and was worn by noncommissioned officers. The 1841 Regulation white buff belt with the same plate was used infrequently early in the war.

Some state troops wore a distinctive plate rather than the oval U.S. plate. Oval plates with SNY (State of New York) and OVM (Ohio Volunteer Militia) were issued in some quantity. A smaller VMM (Volunteer Militia Maine) plate was issued to some units from that state and oval plates bearing the great seal of the states of Maryland and Pennsylvania were also issued in limited quantities.

Cavalryman's belt.   Foot trooper's belt, 1861-1863.   Foot trooper's belt with brass keeper, M1863.   Light artilleryman's belt.

NCO's waist belt and plate.

Militia uniform waist belt and plate.

Foot musician's and NCO's belt.

MUSKETS, RIFLE-MUSKETS, RIFLES AND CARBINES

WITH THE OUTBREAK of hostilities in 1861 there were about 525,000 obsolete Model 1816 and 1840 .69 caliber muskets stored in armories around the country. Most had been altered to the percussion system between 1855 and 1860, and some were even rifled and sighted, but a number were still flintlock. Confederate forces quickly took over all weapons in southern repositories. Those in the North were issued just as quickly to the volunteer army being assembled, particularly the western units. Also at the beginning of the war there were some 167,000 Model 1842 muskets, .69 caliber, in storage. Some of these were also rifled and sighted but some were veterans of the War with Mexico. All of these that had not been confiscated by Southern states were issued to volunteers.

Federal agents were immediately dispatched to the arms markets in England and other European countries to purchase available arms. Many of the Austrian, Belgian and Prussian muskets acquired were as obsolete as the smoothbore muskets available in North America. Nevertheless, they too usually went to the western troops.

The Model 1855 rifle-musket adopted was the first longarm of .58 caliber to fire the Minie bullet. Some 60,000 of these arms were fabricated at Springfield and Harpers Ferry Armories before the war but had already become obsolete by 1860. The most typical of all Civil War arms was the Model 1861 rifle-musket manufactured at Springfield Armory and by more than twenty contractors in

Model 1842 smoothbore musket.

Model 1842 rifled and sighted musket.

Model 1841 rifle.

the Northeast. Almost 1,000,000 were fabricated during the war, 265,129 being made at Springfield. This arm eliminated the troublesome Maynard tape priming system of the Model 1855 and became the epitome of the muzzle-loading percussion rifle-musket.

A Special Model 1861 rifle-musket was introduced, and over 156,000 of the type were made, many of them by the Colt Patent Firearms Company. Over 500,000 Model 1863 rifle-muskets were manufactured with two variations but most of these guns were received too late in the war to see much field service.

Federal arms agents did have some notable success in England. During the war years some 500,000 Pattern 1853 Enfield rifle-muskets, .577 caliber, were imported by the Ordnance Department, Northern states and Northern speculators. This weapon was second only to the Model 1861 rifle-musket in the hands of the soldiers and was well liked by all who carried one.

Rifles were originally issued to flank companies of infantry regiments, but in the Civil War whole regiments were issued the arms. The Model 1841 rifle was manufactured at Harpers Ferry from 1846 until 1855. Over 25,000 were manufactured there, and another 45,500 were made by E. Remington, of Herkimer, New York; Robbins, Kendall and Lawrence and later, Robbins and Lawrence, of Windsor, Vermont; and Tryon in Philadelphia. Many were altered and upgraded between 1855 and

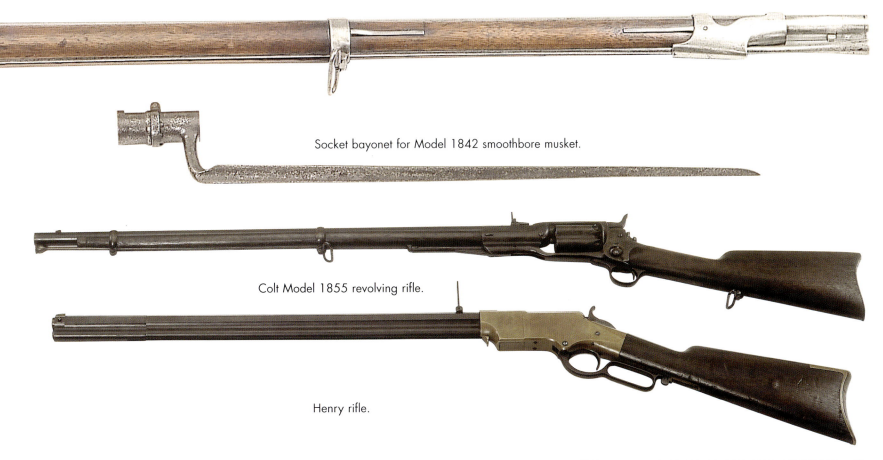

Socket bayonet for Model 1842 smoothbore musket.

Colt Model 1855 revolving rifle.

Henry rifle.

MUSKETS, RIFLE-MUSKETS, RIFLES AND CARBINES

Muskets, Rifle-muskets, Rifles and Carbines

1860 by re-rifling to .58 caliber, adding a long-range rear sight, bayonet adapters, and new steel ramrods. It was considered the most handsome of all U.S. percussion rifles.

The Model 1855 rifle was made in limited quantities, with only 7,317 fabricated at Harpers Ferry. It had the distinction of being the last muzzle-loading rifle manufactured at a national armory. Confederates captured many late production rifles at the beginning of the war.

Other American-made rifles were purchased and used in smaller quantities. The U.S. Navy bought 1,000 Jenks Navy rifles before the war; these had a mule ear side hammer, the only such weapon purchased by the government. In addition, 10,000 .69 caliber Plymouth rifles were purchased for use on board ships.

By far the most technologically advanced weapons were the Henry and Spencer rifles. Both were tube magazine-fed and lever-operated, a giant step forward. They fired self-contained waterproof rimfire cartridges. Of some 14,000 Henrys manufactured, the Ordnance Department bought about 1,700 and they were issued to the 1st Maine and 1st DC Cavalry Regiments. Many others were purchased privately at soldiers' own expense because of their advanced design and firepower. The Army and Navy purchased over 12,000 Spencers. While neither rifle changed the course of history, both foretold the firepower of weapons of the future.

Sharps "New Model" 1859 rifle.

Spencer breechloading rifle.

Greene rifle.

Both Army and Navy purchased the Sharps rifle, Models 1859 and 1863. The Army bought about 10,000 plus 2000 special set trigger rifles for the 1st and 2nd U.S. Sharpshooters. The Navy acquired at least 2,800. This breechloading rifle fired a prepared cartridge and was one of the most reliable and popular arms of the war.

More than 200,000 Austrian Lorenz Rifles, Model 1854 and 14,000 British Pattern 1856 and 1858 Short rifles accounted for the bulk of imported rifles, although small quantities of current and obsolescent Belgian and French rifles have been noted.

In the final analysis the Model 1861 rifle-musket, British Pattern 1853 rifle-musket and Austrian Model 1854 Lorenz rifle were the weapons most likely found in the hands of the Federal soldier.

All cavalry carbines that saw extensive service during the war were breechloading firearms using a specific cartridge. Unfortunately, the government adopted at least seventeen different models. All fired non-interchangeable ammunition. Thus, a tactical advantage became an ordnance supply nightmare. Furthermore, even companies within a regiment were often armed with different-make carbines requiring specific ammunition. Standardization was never achieved during the war but the effect of overwhelming fire superiority was not lost on those who would fight later wars.

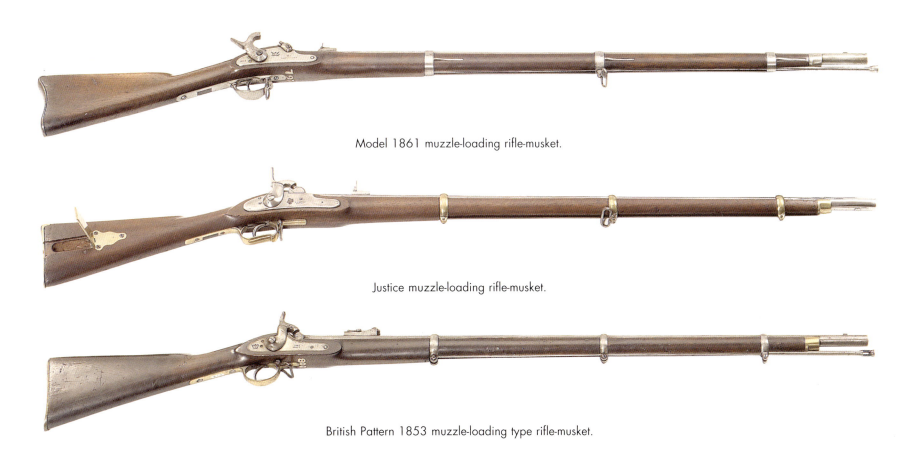

Model 1861 muzzle-loading rifle-musket.

Justice muzzle-loading rifle-musket.

British Pattern 1853 muzzle-loading type rifle-musket.

Muskets, Rifle-muskets, Rifles and Carbines

The Spencer carbine was a magazine-fed and lever-actuated breechloader of great ingenuity. The first Spencers were received in October 1863 and by the end of the war, large numbers of Federal cavalry were armed with them. Total government procurement was 95,181. The Sharps carbine was the most famous single-shot carbine of the war. It used a unique .52 caliber linen cartridge. The Ordnance Department purchased 77,330 New Model 1859 and Model 1863 carbines, and had few negative reports.

The Burnside carbine, 2nd, 3rd and 4th Models, used a peculiar .54 caliber ice cream cone shaped metallic cartridge. The Ordnance Department purchased 53,031 of them and they were extensively used, and criticized by many to whom they were issued. Buford's Cavalry was armed with some Smith carbines the first day of the battle of Gettysburg. The Smith used a .50 caliber rubber cartridge later replaced by a foil round. The large spring at the breech tended to break in use. The government purchased 31,002, as well as 17,728 Gallagher percussion carbines, whose major drawback was the lack of an extractor to remove the fired cartridge.

In addition to these five types various quantities of Starr, Maynard, Remington, Merrill, Joslyn, Gwyn and Campbell, Hall, Warner, Ballard, Sharps and Hankins, Gibbs, Lindner and Wesson carbines were purchased.

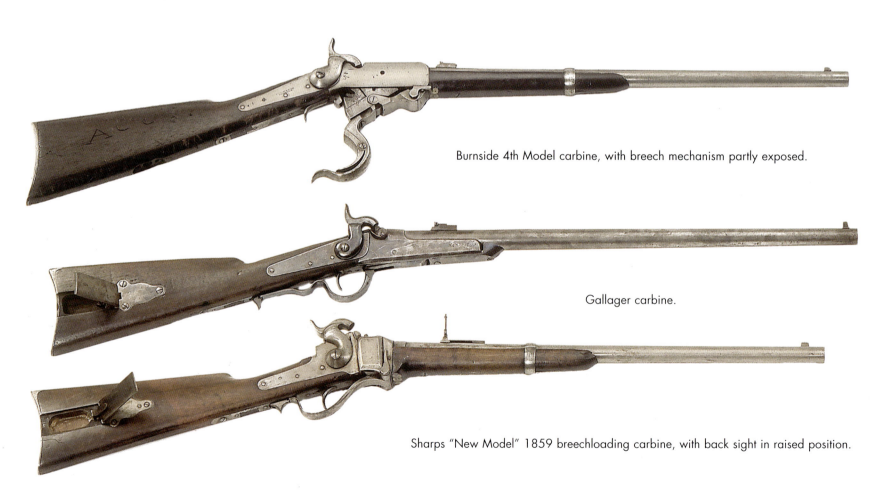

Burnside 4th Model carbine, with breech mechanism partly exposed.

Gallager carbine.

Sharps "New Model" 1859 breechloading carbine, with back sight in raised position.

Spencer carbine with breech mechanism partly exposed and back sight raised.

Smith carbine "broken" to permit reloading.

Maynard 1st Model carbine "broken" for reloading.

Merrill late model carbine with breech open for reloading.

Joslyn Model 1864 carbine.

Starr carbine.

MUSKETS, RIFLE-MUSKETS, RIFLES AND CARBINES

Pistols and Revolvers

The Federal Government purchased just fewer than 400,000 handguns during the war for officers of all branches, cavalry troops, and mounted artillery personnel. The most popular calibers were .36 Navy and .44 Army. The total purchased officially did not include, of course, the private purchase of handguns by individual officers and enlisted men. However, the infantryman, after a twenty-mile forced march, quickly realized he didn't need the extra encumbrance of a handgun, no matter how small, and such weapons were promptly sold, sent home or discarded. Therefore, handguns were used in relatively limited numbers compared to the longarms of the infantrymen, who made up the great bulk of the army.

The predominant manufacturer of handguns at the beginning of the war was the Colt Patent Firearms Company. Samuel Colt had carefully developed contacts within the Ordnance procurement

Massachusetts Arms Company Adams Patent Navy revolver.

Colt Model 1851 Navy revolver, .36 caliber.

Colt New Model Army 1860 revolver, .44 caliber

94 EQUIPMENT OF THE FEDERAL FORCES

Remington New Model Army revolver.

Remington-Beals Navy revolver.

Remington New Model Navy revolver.

Starr Army revolver.

Pistols and Revolvers

Whitney Navy revolver.

Manhattan Pocket Model revolver.

Plant Third Model revolver.

Colt Model 1862 Police revolver.

bureaucracy to insure predominance of his products. Ordnance Department and open market purchases of the Colt Model 1860 Army revolver amounted to 129,375 pieces. Some 35,000 Colt Model 1851 Navy revolvers were bought by the government and there were certainly other state purchases. Federal military units were issued nearly 165,000 Colt handguns. It has been estimated that 80 percent of Federal cavalry was armed with the Model 1860 Colt Army revolver at some point during service.

Second to Colt was E. Remington and Sons of Ilion, New York. This company furnished Beals-Remington, Remington Old Model and New Model Revolvers in .36 and .44 caliber. It is estimated that the government purchased about 137,500 Remington pieces, primarily after stopping orders with

Colt Model 1860 Army revolver, fluted barrel.

Smith & Wesson No. 2 Army revolver.

Smith & Wesson No. 1 Second Issue revolver.

PISTOLS AND REVOLVERS 97

Pistols and Revolvers

Colt in November 1863 because Remington and others were less expensive. These solid frame revolvers were rugged and reliable.

The Starr Arms Company was the third largest supplier of double action and single action revolvers in both calibers, with total sales to the government of nearly 48,000 revolvers. The Model 1861 double action revolver was delicate and prone to malfunction in the field. The Model 1863 single action was simpler and more efficient but still not liked by troops that carried them.

The Ordnance Department acquired nearly 17,500 Whitney Navy revolvers. Over 11,000 were issued to western army units with nearly 6,300 used by the Federal Navy. About 12,000 of the Savage Navy Revolvers were purchased, despite the ungainly appearance and fragility.

Colt Model 1849 Pocket revolver.

Colt Model 1860 Army revolver.

Colt Model 1849 Pocket revolver.

Butterfield Percussion Army revolver, .41 caliber.

Joslyn Army revolver, .44 caliber.

Pettengill Army revolver, .44 caliber.

Starr Model 1858 Navy revolver, .36 caliber.

PISTOLS AND REVOLVERS 99

Pistols and Revolvers

Allen & Wheelock Lipfire Army revolver, .44 caliber.

Starr Model 1863 Army revolver, .44 caliber.

Savage-North Navy revolver, .36 caliber.

Perrin and Company revolver, .45 caliber.

These five makers supplied almost 380,000 revolvers of almost 400,000 purchased. Other revolvers were in limited use and evidence exists indicating that soldiers were armed with Adams, Allen and Wheelock, Butterfield, Freeman, Joslyn, Manhattan, Pettengill, Prescott, and Smith and Wesson No. 2 Army Revolvers. Foreign handguns such as the LeFaucheux pinfire, Perrin, and Raphael played minor roles. Some of these revolvers have appeared in contemporary photography.

There were about 42,000 obsolete Model 1842 single-shot pistols in government storage and an unknown number of Model 1836 pistols, some still in flint but most altered to percussion, and some saw limited use in the early months of the war. Almost any handgun of the period might have been carried off to war by an enthusiastic volunteer but, on the field of battle, the majority of handguns were Colt and Remington revolvers.

Colt Model 1848 Army revolver, 1st Model, .44 caliber.

Freeman Army Model revolver, .44 caliber.

LeFaucheaux revolver, 1853.

CARTRIDGE BOXES

THE CAP BOX and cartridge box were primary components of the set of accouterments most soldiers wore throughout the war to carry ammunition for their firearm. These items were supplied by the Ordnance Department and were manufactured at several government arsenals and many civilian contractors. In practice, complete sets of accouterments, cap and cartridge boxes, waist and shoulder belts with plates and bayonet scabbards, were delivered. Between January 1861 and June 1865 more than of 2,100,000 sets of infantry accouterments were purchased.

The cartridge boxes used during the war included several patterns. The primary difference was size dictated by the ammunition carried, either .69 or .58 caliber. Boxes most often encountered were the Patterns of 1857, 1861, March 1864 and July 1864, although older patterns were issued early in the war. The July 1864 Pattern eliminated the brass oval "US" box plate that had been affixed to the cartridge box for over twenty years; it was replaced with a "US" embossed on the leather flap.

M1855 .69 caliber cavalry pistol cartridge box.

M1839 .69 caliber cartridge box with sling.

M1855 .58 caliber rifle-musket cartridge box.

M1864 .69 caliber cartridge box.

102 EQUIPMENT OF THE FEDERAL FORCES

CARTRIDGE BOXES 103

Firearms Tools and Accessories

THE CAP BOX, like the cartridge box, evolved through a series of improvements. Early cap boxes had sewn straps only. Later boxes utilized brass rivets to reinforce stitching. The face of the cap box changed from a shield shape to one that completely covered the box with sewn latch tab.

A rifle box and several carbine boxes were also produced, as well as a set of accouterments for the Navy with boxes embossed with letters "USN".

The percussion cap was absolutely essential in the firing of any percussion arm. These small copper caps contained a combustible compound that was ignited by the strike of the hammer on the cone where the cap was seated. This fire was communicated down through the cone into the chamber of the barrel and ignited the cartridge. Some weapons such as the Sharps were fitted with a mechanical priming device and the primers were used in place of the cap. Other tools were necessary to maintain the

Circa 1861 cap box.

Percussion cap box with percussion caps as issued.

Circa 1863/1864 cap box.

104   EQUIPMENT OF THE FEDERAL FORCES

individual weapon. There was a gun wrench that had a screwdriver head and cone wrench; this was standard with the musket, rifle-musket and rifle. These muzzle-loading weapons also had a worm and ball puller that screwed onto the reverse end of the ramrod and enabled the soldier to pull an old round out of the barrel and to clean out any residue. Most revolvers had specific tools like the L-shaped screwdriver and cone wrench for Colt and Remington revolvers. The various carbines all had unique, specific tools. A main spring vise was issued to NCOs to assist in the stripping of the lock under supervision.

Bullet molds were issued in some quantity to enable bullets to be cast in the field if necessary. These molds were made in handgun and longarm calibers in either brass or iron with single or multiple cavities.

Pistol bullet mold device.

Tools for use with rifle-muskets.

Pistol tool for Colt Model 1860 Army revolver.

Powder flask for recharging individual chambers of revolver.

Powder flask.

Non-regulation holster for Colt revolver.

Remington revolver holster.

FIREARMS TOOLS AND ACCESSORIES

Edged Weapons

BELOW RIGHT: Ohio cavalrymen, such as these with their regular issue sabers with three-bar type of grip guards, came to typify the look of the rugged western Yankees who filled the ranks of the Union cavalry. Young, lean, with few frills, they were tough business in the saddle.

FEDERAL OFFICERS AND NCOs of all branches and mounted troops carried edged weapons of different patterns. Most were copies of French weapons. The most common enlisted men's edged weapons were the Model 1840 and Model 1860 cavalry saber, the Model 1840 light artillery saber, Model 1832 foot artillery sword, Model 1860 naval cutlass and the Model 1840 NCOs' sword, and the Model 1840 musicians' sword. These swords were brass mounted, plain and functional. The Ames Manufacturing Company, C. Roby and Co., and Sheble and Fisher made most under contract to the Ordnance Department.

Officers' edged weapons were more ornate and had become primarily a badge of rank by the mid-19th century. The Model 1850 foot officers' sword was carried by Company grade officers,

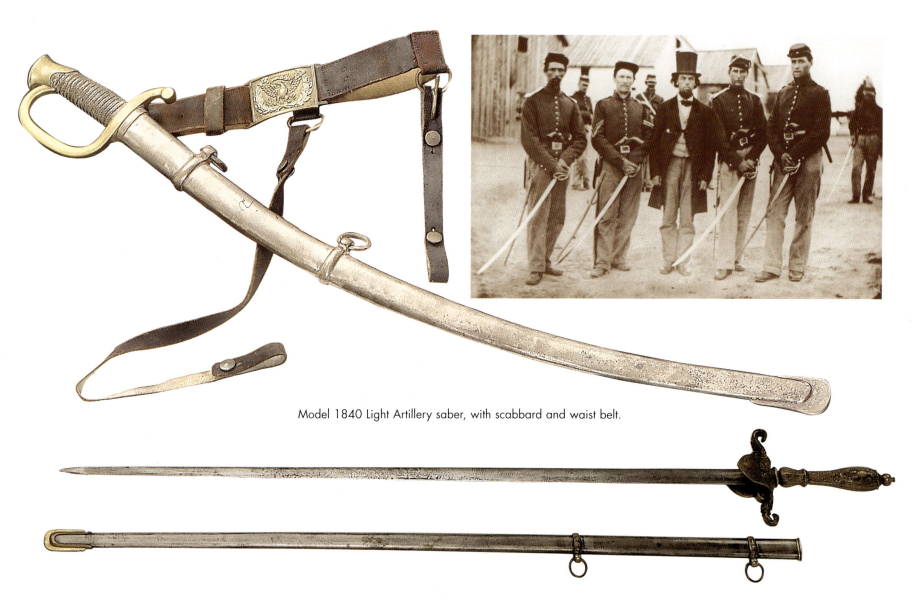

Model 1840 Light Artillery saber, with scabbard and waist belt.

Model 1840 medical officer's sword, with scabbard.

106 EQUIPMENT OF THE FEDERAL FORCES

Model 1840 cavalry saber with three-bar grip guard, with scabbard.

Model 1840 regulation foot officer's sword, with scabbard.

Model 1840 cavalry officer's sabre, with scabbard.

Model 1850 staff and field officer's sword, with scabbard.

EDGED WEAPONS 107

Edged Weapons

Model 1850 foot officer's sword, with brass-mounted leather scabbard.

Model 1850 foot officer's sword, with all german silver scabbard.

Imported Model 1840 design of cavalry saber with hilt in iron, and scabbard.

Model 1860 cavalry saber with three-bar grip guard, and scabbard.

lieutenants and captains; the Model 1850 staff and field officers' sword was authorized for majors, colonels and general officers. The Model 1860 staff and field officers' sword, much lighter, was also authorized and saw some service. Cavalry and artillery officers' sabers were more elaborate and higher quality of the same pattern as carried by enlisted personnel. The Navy used the Model 1852 sword for all officers.

There were a considerable number of non-regulation officers' swords and sabers imported from Soligen, the blade capital of Europe, and a lesser number from France and England. Most generally followed the authorized patterns but some were quite unusual.

Model 1860 staff and field officer's sword, with scabbard.

Model 1860 cavalry officer's saber, with scabbard.

ABOVE: A general with his staff, each armed with a sword for use rather than dress: Brigadier General Edwin V. Sumner, with distinctive white beard, was the oldest active general officer of the war, commanding II Corps of the Army of Potomac in the 1862 Peninsular Campaign, and Burnside's Left Grand Division at Fredricksburg. He died in March 1863, aged sixty-six, on his way to a new command in the West. On his left is his son, Lt. Samuel S. Sumner.

Bayonet Frogs and Scabbards

All muskets, rifle muskets, and most rifles were designed to accept a triangular (mostly) or saber bayonet. Triangular bayonets were used on muskets and rifle-muskets. Some rifles such as the Sharps and Spencer were manufactured in two configurations for either a triangular socket bayonet or brass-hilted saber bayonet. When not attached to the firearms, bayonets were carried in brass-mounted leather scabbards that had an integral leather frog in the case of most socket bayonets or were attached to a separate frog, as for most saber bayonets. The frog held the bayonet scabbard and had a belt loop, enabling the bayonet to be carried on the waist belt when not in use. Bayonet scabbards and frogs were made in the U.S., and also imported for foreign bayonets.

Model 1855 saber bayonet frog.

Frog for swords and sword bayonets.

Cap box, waist belt and bayonet scabbard.

Scabbard for bayonet below

Socket bayonet.

Socket-type bayonet, scabbard and frog.

Model 1855 rifleman's waist belt and saber bayonet.   Model 1859 bayonet scabbard for imports.   Model 1859 U.S. bayonet scabbard.   Model 1863 bayonet scabbard.

BAYONET FROGS AND SCABBARDS 111

Haversacks and Knapsacks

THE HAVERSACK AND knapsack were Quartermaster Department issue items and every foot soldier carried them in some form. Before and during the war millions were fabricated but most were worn out in service. Survival rate was low and extant specimens are rare.

The haversack was a basic black-painted canvas weatherproof bag with shoulder strap. It was used primarily for carrying food rations and necessary items not stored in the knapsack. A cotton inner sack was ineffectually utilized to prevent grease soiling the uniform. Size was about eleven by twelve inches, and the haversack was conveniently carried on the left hip usually under the canteen. Haversacks were often carried by officers but in such instances were private purchase items, sometimes of hand tooled, fine quality leather.

The knapsack carried all the soldier's gear that wasn't worn on his person. Early in the war much unnecessary impedimenta was carried by the volunteer but was discarded along the route of the first hard march, or sent home shortly thereafter. A shelter half and rubber blanket were carried rolled and strapped to the top of the knapsack. The overcoat, when carried, was neatly folded and carried under the knapsack flap. Within the knapsack were found necessary personal items such as a "housewife" containing needles, thread and spare buttons, razor, comb, tooth brush, soap and towel, Bible,

Artillery haversack.   Standard issue enlisted man's haversack with inner (rice) bag.   Officer's purchase leather haversack.

112 EQUIPMENT OF THE FEDERAL FORCES

combination knife, fork and spoon, candle holder, paper and envelopes, extra socks and underwear. Some soldiers included a deck of cards.

The militia hardpack knapsack, with wooden frame covered by painted cloth, was seen early in the war. Pattern 1855 and 1864 double bag soft knapsacks were standard toward the end of the conflict. Many non-regulation or patent knapsacks were purchased by state agents or individual units and were limited issue items.

Model 1855 standard-issue bag pattern knapsack.

Model 1855 bag pattern knapsack with soldier-painted unit designation.

Patent gutta-percha type knapsack, box pattern, 137th NY.

Box pattern knapsack, 7th Regiment NY State Militia.

HAVERSACKS AND KNAPSACKS

Canteens and Mess Gear

After decades of experimentation with wood, rubber, leather, and tin drum canteens the Federal Government adopted the Model 1858 tin canteen as the regulation service canteen for all personnel. This canteen was an oblate spheroid pattern of two circular sections soldered together at the common rim. Diameter was about 7½ inches and width at the center about 2½ inches. Capacity was about three pints of liquid. There were three tin loops soldered around the edge for attachment of a white cotton or leather shoulder strap. The spout was pewter and soldered to the top edge of the canteen. The body of the canteen was covered with blue, gray or brown wool or cotton stitched around the edge.

The Quartermaster Department contracted with civilian tinsmiths for tens of thousands of these canteens. Many of these contract canteens had concentric rings pressed into both sides for strength, and these were known as bullseye canteens. Limited numbers of canteens were made of copper and pewter. Some private purchase filter and other patent device canteens were purchased by officers and men.

Every man carried some sort of canteen at all times. Many have been recovered from wartime sites with the solder melted in order to use the halves as plates.

Model 1858 canteen with non-standard cloth strap.

Model 1858 canteen made late war by New York contractor.

Model 1862 ringed-body canteen with strap over knapsack and bed roll.

Non-standard pattern, tin-drum canteen with screw top.

Non-regulation Bartholomew's Patent Water Filtration Canteen.

There are Confederate copies of this very utilitarian piece of equipment. The pattern remained standard with the U.S. Army into the 20th century. It has been said that an army travels on its stomach, so a soldier had to be fed. During the Civil War small groups of soldiers banded together in informal messes and prepared their own meals when rations and time allowed. Each mess had some cooking equipment such as a large coffee tin pot, iron skillet, some assorted tin pots, plates, boilers and possibly a basin, some knives, dippers and sieves. Canteen halves were known to substitute as plates. Most of the larger equipment was carried in company wagons and not always accessible.

The individual soldier always had a tin cup, part of Pattern 1851 equipment. A spoon, pocket knife, combination folding knife, fork and spoon, or other patent eating utensil were carried in his pocket or haversack. All of these items were probably purchased from the unit sutler. Even on the march he had the necessary eating instruments.

Officers often had more elaborate mess equipment with complete sets of plates and eating utensils carried in large chests. This was particularly true of higher ranks. Liquor and wine sets were part of this equipage and a fine table was sometimes set.

Standard issue pattern canteen cup.

Canteen cup with bail handle.

Mess kit for attachment to rear of knapsack.

Folding cup.

Tin plate, spoon, hardtack, and utensils.

Coffee pot.

Miscellaneous Accouterments

This potpourri of accouterments from varying ranks and branches of service includes the predominant saddle in use during the Civil War, the Model 1859 McClellan saddle for officers and enlisted men. Officers' saddles were usually modified with a quilted seat and finer tack such as matching bridle, saddle holsters and saddlebags, and were dressed with a fine shabraque. Other popular saddles were the Hope and Jennifer patterns.

Officers and signal unit personnel carried optics. Both monocular and binocular types were popular. Most binoculars were imported from France though a small number were made in North America.

The Quartermaster Department supplied wool army blankets, and state contractors supplied many of lesser quality. Most have a "US" embroidered in the center.

Brass spurs, issued and private purchase, were worn by most mounted personnel.

Model 1859 Officer's McLellan saddle (of Major General John Sedgwick), with pair of saddle revolver holsters, Martingale or breast strap with brass presentation plaque, saddle valise at rear for stowage of articles and clothing and other items, saddle bags, general officer's shabraque or saddle covering with insignia of major general, sweat leathers to prevent soiling of rider's uniform, and stirrups and hoods for protection of rider's feet.

Saddle on which Major General John F. Reynolds was shot and killed, together with sword belt and sash.

Pair of brass spurs.

Pair of cavalryman's field glasses.

Pair of binoculars that belonged to Major General George G. Meade.

Officer's monocular glass.

Artillery fuze pouch and belt.

Artillery blanket.

Non-standard soldier's blanket.

Non-standard blanket, but marked "US."

MISCELLANEOUS ACCOUTERMENTS 117

Musical Instruments and Accouterments

BANDS AND MARTIAL music have long inspired patriotism and fighting spirit. By the mid-19th century military bands played an important part in the popular militia system throughout the country. The bands of the Civil War were composed almost entirely of brass and percussion instruments and found at regimental and brigade level. Everyday military life was directed by company or regimental bugle-, drum-, and fife-directed calls. Commands for reveille, drill, and meals were given by musical instrument. Federal and Confederate armies were authorized by regulations to have two field musicians per company, a drummer and fifer for infantry and bugler for cavalry. These field musicians formed a regimental drum corps commanded by a drum major, a non-commissioned officer. Bands

Saxhorn brass instrument.

Pair of drumsticks with carrier and body harness.

Bugle with lanyard.

Band leader's baton.

118 EQUIPMENT OF THE FEDERAL FORCES

Fife made of rosewood.

Model 1845 French infantry bugle carried by G. W. Freeman, Co. H, 62nd Pennsylvania Volunteer Infantry (Zouaves).

Bugle with attachment points for lanyard.

Eagle style snare drum and pair of drumsticks.

MUSICAL INSTRUMENTS AND ACCOUTERMENTS 119

Musical Instruments and Accouterments

BELOW: A fife and drum corps of an unidentified regiment. Drummers had distinctive white support straps. Here, the musicians with fifes have them tucked under their left arms.

played for parades, guard mount, morning colors, reviews and funerals. During battle bandsmen served as stretcher-bearers and surgeons' assistants in hospital. After the battle they gathered and buried the dead.

Invariably, the bands marched at the front of the column to facilitate the use of the over-the-shoulder horns, enabling the music to flow back over the column. The instruments were primarily various brass horns and wood shell drums. Base and snare drums were the basic types and army records indicate more than 3,200 were purchased during the war. Associated accouterments were slings, beaters, and sticks. The bulk of horns were privately owned and brought into military service.

Key type of bugle.

Model 1840 musician's long sword with scabbard and shoulder harness belt.

120 EQUIPMENT OF THE FEDERAL FORCES

Regulation drums from New York, Vermont, and Massachusetts regiments.

MUSICAL INSTRUMENTS AND ACCOUTERMENTS 121

National And Unit Flags

During the Civil War the unit flags were the soul of the regiment, guarded by men specially chosen for stature and previous valor at great personal risk, the rallying point in time of crisis and the focal point of fire from opposing forces. There were garrison and storm flags for permanent stations, headquarters and designating flags for armies, corps, divisions and brigades, regimental and company flags, flank guides for regiments, and ships' flags.

Most regimental flags were made of silk and consisted of a national flag, the stars and stripes, and a regimental color, an eagle on a blue ground for infantry and crossed cannon on a yellow ground for artillery. Regulation flags were six feet by six feet. Many state colors had the state coat of arms worked

State national color purchased by officers of 50th Pennsylvania Volunteer Infantry to replace flag lost at Battle of Second Manassas (Second Bull Run), August 29-30, 1862.

Camp color of 99th Pennsylvania Volunteer Infantry. Red diamond indicates that the regiment was assigned to 1st Division, 3rd Corps; blue strip signified that the regiment was part of the 2nd Brigade of that division.

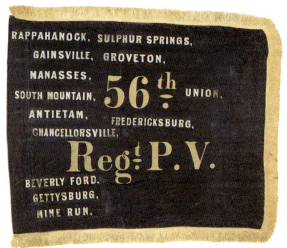

Camp color of 56th Pennsylvania Volunteer Infantry, bearing battle honors and trimmed with gold fringe.

122 EQUIPMENT OF THE FEDERAL FORCES

State regimental color, 138th Pennsylvania Volunteer Infantry (Christmas 1864) during siege of Petersburg.

National and Unit Flags

into the canton on the national flag or substituted for the eagle on the regimental color. Flank guides were sometimes of silk but often made of wool bunting, and marked the flank of the regiment when the unit was in line of battle. Most larger station, ship and headquarters flags were of wool bunting.

Early in the war many volunteer companies received presentation flags crafted by ladies of their area, but these flags were retired by the second year of the war. Later, some regiments received finely

HQ designation flag of the 2nd Brigade, 2nd Division, 2nd Army Corps, Army of the Potomac, commanded by Brigadier General Alexander Stewart Webb.

Swallow-tail camp color of 91st Pennsylvania Volunteer Infantry. The flag is non-regulation in shape, but features a white field in accordance with regulations of 1836.

State guidon of Company G, 1st Pennsylvania Cavalry, made by Holtsmann Brother and Company, Philadelphia. Note Pennsylvania State coat of arms on the top.

embroidered presentation colors but such flags were rarely carried in harm's way.

Companies such as Horstmann and Evans and Hassall in Philadelphia, Tiffany's in New York, and Sisco Brothers in Baltimore manufactured fine presentation colors which did see the smoke of battle, but most combat colors were fabricated according to Army regulations by private contractors for the Cincinnati, New York, and Philadelphia Quartermaster Depots.

National guidon of Company I, 6th Pennsylvania Cavalry, with battle honors inscribed.

NATIONAL AND UNIT FLAGS 125

Equipment of the Confederate Forces

ABOVE: A CSA plate as issued to troops in the Eastern Theater.

LEFT: Having to contend with hotter climates, these men of the 9th Mississippi near Pensacola in 1861 have erected a brush-covered arbor, called a "shebang," between their tents, to protect them from the sun. The Confederates were generally more impoverished than their Federal counterparts.

OFFICERS' COATS AND JACKETS

THE 1861 REGULATION Confederate officers' coat was based on a contemporary Austrian tunic that was double-breasted with two rows of seven buttons, a standing collar and a skirt that reached half way between the hip and the knee, considerably shorter than a conventional frock coat. Colored facings and piping, buff for staff, red for artillery, yellow for cavalry, blue for infantry and black for medical, indicated branch of service. The Austrian tunic was short-lived and the familiar frock coat became standard in 1862 because it was comfortable and practical.

Confederate officers' coats and uniforms in general were inspired by regulations but dictated by taste, tailor and finances. For the Confederate volunteer officer the specifications of formal Army Regulations meant very little. His uniform was the product of what material was available and the

Pleated-front uniform blouse of Lieutenant General Simon Bolivar Buckner.

Uniform blouse of General Braxton Bragg, in accordance with regulations but with buttons in pairs rather than equi-distant.

Uniform blouse of General Pierre G. T. Beauregard, with non-regulation epaulets and unique belt plate.

General Rosser's uniform coat, front and rear.

Uniform blouse with sash of General John Bell Hood, with buttons in threes.

OFFICERS' COATS AND JACKETS 129

Officers' Coats and Jackets

talents of the local tailor. Officers' frock coats were made in both single and double-breasted patterns, which was not regulation. Branch of service colors were used on cuffs and collar of some, while others had only branch of service piping. Some coats had no branch indication whatsoever.

Officers' shell jackets also appeared in both single- and double-breasted patterns with the same almost random attention to regulations. This pattern became very popular because it was easy to make

Frock coat of
Brigadier General Paul Semmes.

Frock coat of
Major General Joseph Wheeler.

Frock coat of
Lieutenant General John Bell Hood.

and used less material, and was therefore less expensive.

The Confederate Navy Regulations of 1862 stipulated a gray frock coat for officers. This was a radical departure from custom of the use of blue for all naval uniforms.

Galloons or Austrian knots, the arrangement of gold sleeve braid, denoted rank after the fashion of undress uniforms of the French officer corps. Other uniforms had subdued galloons, abbreviated

Frock coat of Major General Frank Gardner.

Frock coat of Lieutenant General Simon Bolivar Buckner (see also page 128).

Frock coat of Brigadier General George Wythe Randolph. Secretary of War.

OFFICERS' COATS AND JACKETS 131

Officers' Coats and Jackets

galloons or galloons in branch of service color. As an alternative to galloons, some uniforms had a strip of gold lace running from cuff to elbow decorated with small ball buttons. Officers' frock coats have been noted devoid of all rank insignia, an approach way ahead of the times in an effort to avoid presenting ranking targets to snipers. A buff silk sash was proscribed for all general officers and a dark maroon silk sash for other officer ranks

Collar insignia also denoted rank. General officers wore three stars surrounded by an embroidered wreath on both sides of the collar. Colonels wore three stars, lieutenant colonels two and majors one. Captains wore three bars, first lieutenants two and second lieutenants one. Collars varied greatly from the proscribed stand-up pattern and falling collars and rolled collars have been noted with variations of this rank insignia affixed.

Material utilized in confederate officers' coats was diverse. English broadcloth, wool jean, wool and cotton blends, homespun wool and wool kersey have all been noted. As with other Quartermaster items, huge quantities of fine gray material were imported from England. Uniform material made in the Confederacy varied in quality and color, running the gamut from dark gray to butternut.

Artillery officer's uniform coat, front and rear. Quartermaster's uniform coat of Hutson Lee, front and rear.

Officers' Hats and Caps

CONFEDERATE UNIFORM REGULATIONS authorized the wear of the forage cap for all officers and were specific, enumerating colors for branch of service and number of strands of gold lace utilized in quatrefoil. Officers purchased their own headgear and tailors had their own interpretation of regulations, so an officer's forage cap fabricated to quartermaster specifications was unusual, although many did exist.

The regulations also authorized the chapeau for optional dress. While officers who served in the Federal army may have retained that type of headgear from previous service there was no evidence of

Tassled beret worn by General Pierre G. T. Beauregard.

Slouch hat worn by General Robert E. Lee.

General Beauregard's kepi.

High-topped forage cap of General Thomas Jonathan Jackson.

Plumed felt hat of General J. E. B. Stuart, made in Paris, and certainly non-regulation.

Forage cap of Brigadier General George Wythe Randolph.

Officers' Hats and Caps

Confederate manufacture.

Artillery officers were directed to wear a forage cap of red wool with leather visor. Cavalry officers wore yellow and infantry wore blue. In actuality, sometimes the top of the hat was made of branch of service color material and other times a band of branch of service color material encircled the hat.

The latitude allowed officers in their clothing appeared immeasurable. Many decided to forgo the forage cap altogether for the much more comfortable and effective slouch hat. Many slouch hats were civilian private purchase hats with gold and black officers' hat cords and any insignia that struck

Forage cap of Brigadier General John B. Magruder.

Forage cap of Lieutenant General Simon Bolivar Buckner.

Forage cap of Brigadier General Paul Semmes.

Model 1858 Hardee hat of Colonel Francis S. Barlow, 7th and 8th Georgia Regiments.

Battered Model 1858 Hardee hat of Captain Paul Hamilton, with North Carolina palmetto insignia and officer's hat cord.

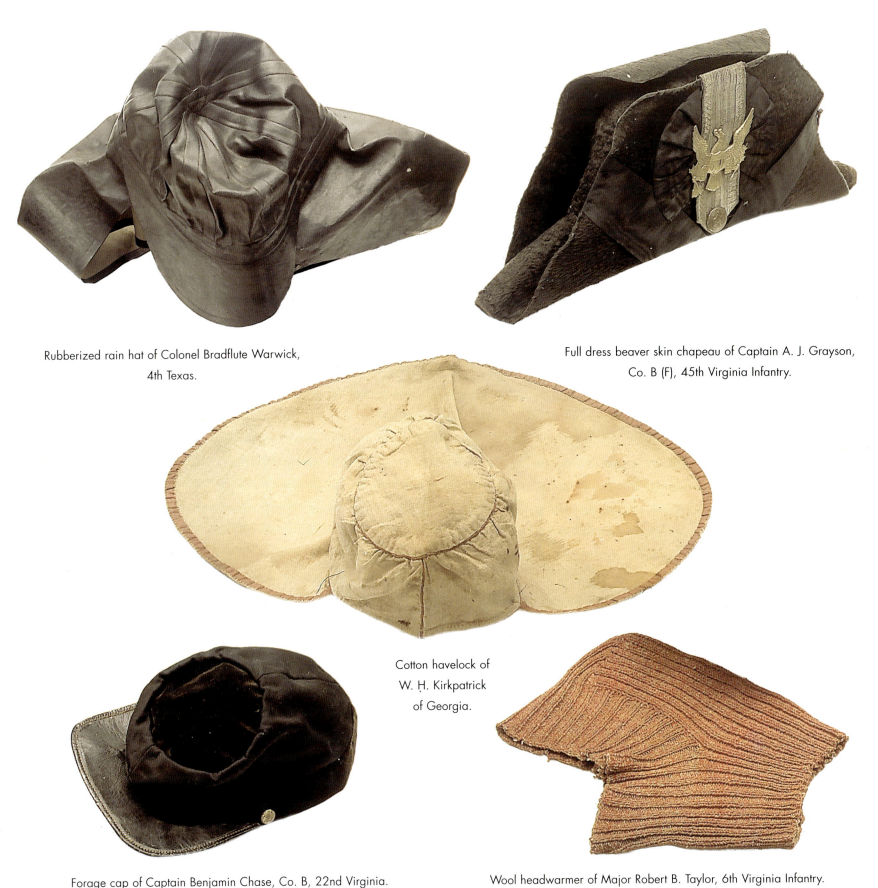

Rubberized rain hat of Colonel Bradflute Warwick, 4th Texas.

Full dress beaver skin chapeau of Captain A. J. Grayson, Co. B (F), 45th Virginia Infantry.

Cotton havelock of W. H. Kirkpatrick of Georgia.

Forage cap of Captain Benjamin Chase, Co. B, 22nd Virginia.

Wool headwarmer of Major Robert B. Taylor, 6th Virginia Infantry.

OFFICERS' HATS AND CAPS 135

Officers' Hats and Caps

the officer's fancy. Specific branch of service insignia was sometimes used. The color and shape of officers' slouch hats appeared to be dictated by taste and availability.

Confederate officers did not shun the appropriation of captured Federal slouch hats, and foul weather gear was worn when available. Non-regulation camp hats were also popular among officers. These were nondescript straw, wool or corduroy hats in some respects similar to modern day baseball caps. Regular straw hats were popular during warmer periods.

Like so many Quartermaster items the headgear regulations were a guide only. Officer preference and financial means were the deciding factors. Replacement headgear was difficult to obtain.

"Butternut" felt officer's hat.

Forage cap of Colonel W. J. Clark, North Carolina troops.

Slouch hat of First Lieutenant W. James Kinchloe.

Forage cap of Captain G. Gaston Otey, Co. A, 13th Battalion, Virginia.

Militia pattern cavalry officer's cap, 6th Battalion, Tennessee Cavalry.

ENLISTED MEN'S COATS AND JACKETS

ALTHOUGH THE SHELL jacket was the standard upper garment, soldiers were also issued frock coats and sack coats. All were made of wool, wool and cotton twill, wool jean cloth or kersey. Some shell jackets were trimmed with branch of service colored tape on collars and cuffs and some units chose a color because it was fashionable. Single-breasted frock coats were worn through the war but were more common in the early years. North Carolina issued distinctive sack coats to state troops and managed to adequately clothe its regiments throughout the war.

Huge quantities of cloth were imported from England, and Peter Tait of Limerick, Ireland, sent bales of ready-made cadet gray kersey uniforms with buttons of his own manufacture through the blockade on his own ships.

Unidentified gray frock coat, front and rear.

Louisiana nine-button frock coat, with state buttons, overlaying Confederate-issue shirt, together with Louisiana shell jacket, pair of white cotton gloves found in pocket of frock coat, framed image of owner of the coat, and storage bag for the framed image. Apparently, the shirt and shell jacket were worn by an English participant in the war.

Enlisted Men's Hats and Caps

REGULATIONS AUTHORIZED THE wear of the forage cap but southern soldiers also wore a variety of slouch hats and palmetto straw hats. Forage caps were made of cotton or wool jean cloth, with brims of leather or oilcloth and chinstraps of similar material. Some were made in branch of service color or had a band of that color, but most were gray or butternut.

Slouch hats came with brims turned up or down, one side pinned up or both sides pinned up, and were adorned with brass, silver, pewter or embroidered insignia at the discretion of the wearer. It seemed no two were alike. Color was usually black or some shade of brown, and the favored insignia was a star or state badge. A substantial number of English slouch hats were imported.

Hardee hat used as slouch hat, recovered from Gettysburg battlefield.

Artilleryman's kepi.

Forage cap typically worn by enlisted gunners.

Alternative style forage cap for enlisted gunners.

Forage cap typically worn by musicians.

138   EQUIPMENT OF THE CONFEDERATE FORCES

Footwear

Large numbers of Federal Jefferson bootees or brogans and Wellington boots were worn by Confederate foot soldiers and mounted troops, and had to work very hard. Capture of quartermaster supplies and the stripping of dead (and sometimes living) Federal troops at every opportunity made these fine brogans and boots available.

Confederate-manufactured brogans copied the same Jefferson pattern and were supplied by many contractors in varying quality to the Quartermaster Department. In addition, significant numbers of officers' boots were civilian private purchases.

England supplied thousands of pairs of shoes to the Confederate fighting man. One pattern was square-toed with hobnail pegs in the soles. Another pattern had buckle closure rather than lace and eyelets. English footwear was admired for its sturdy quality.

Boots of an officer (J. T. McKenna).

Well worn-in infantryman's brogans.

Brogans attributed to an unknown officer.

ENLISTED MEN'S HATS AND CAPS / FOOTWEAR

Waist Belts

Sword belts and waist belts were the two primary types of Confederate belts. The sword belt suspended an edged weapon and was worn by officers of all branches of service, and by mounted troops. The waist belt was an integral part of a set of accouterments and suspended the cap box, cartridge box and bayonet with scabbard.

Sword belts were made of leather or canvas, painted or unpainted, and had two sword hangers affixed. The belt was usually between one-and-one-half inches to two inches wide with brass mountings and was secured by a belt plate. Leather belts were constructed of a single thickness or sometimes folded over a cloth core and sewn on the reverse. Most were black or dark brown although

Militia-style musician's waist belt with metal belt plate.

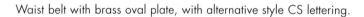

Waist belt with brass oval CS plate.

Waist belt with brass oval plate, with alternative style CS lettering.

Waist belt with brass frame buckle.

140 EQUIPMENT OF THE CONFEDERATE FORCES

white and black enameled examples have been noted.

Waist belts were also made of leather or painted or unpainted canvas and were usually the same width as the sword belt, and similarly were secured by a belt plate. Methods of construction were similar to that used for sword belts, but colors were again normally restricted to the usual black or dark brown.

Both types of belts were fabricated at government arsenals and by many private contractors, and a substantial number were imported along with much other material and weapons from England through the Federal blockade.

Belt with holster and cap box carried by Captain William A. Wright.

Waist belt with brass rectangular C.S.A. belt plate.

Belt with two-piece interlocking Virginia state seal plate belonging to Brigadier General John B. Floyd.

Belt with two-piece interlocking CS plate.

Belt Plates

CONFEDERATE SOLDIERS WORE more than several hundred different styles of belt plates, including brass frame, rectangular, oval, and two-piece interlocking patterns. Substantial numbers were imported from England, while thousands of captured Federal plates were also utilized.

The General Service plates were produced in numerous foundries all over the South. These plates were either generic brass frame buckles in several sizes or sheet brass plates, both generally rectangular in shape, used on both sword and waist belts. Frame buckles were made with forked, double or single tongues. Sheet brass plates had hooks in various configurations soldered to the reverse for belt attachment. These buckles were by far the more common types in Confederate service.

Plate and buckles bearing the letters "CS" or "CSA," state seal or state letter designation were also made in quantity but nowhere near that of General Service plates. Styles were rectangular, oval and two-piece interlocking. Brass, pewter, sheet iron and even precious metal examples have been noted. The rectangular CSA plate fabricated at the Atlanta Arsenal and the two-piece interlocking CS plate made in Richmond were the most common, if any Confederate plate may be called common.

Thousands of snake buckles were imported from England, and there were also English-made plates bearing state seals and the arms of the Confederate States Navy.

Oval Maryland state seal plate.

Maryland state seal sword belt plate.

Oval Mississippi state seal plate.

Alabama state seal sword belt plate.

Oval Alabama state seal plate.

Louisiana state seal plate.

Oval South Carolina plate.

Texas plate.

Oval plate of Alabama Volunteer Corps.

Virginia state seal sword belt plate.

Oval Texas plate.

Virginia state seal sword belt plate.

C.S.A plate, Eastern Theater.

Oval CS plate with beaded border, Western Theater.

CSA rectangular plate, silvered.

CS plate, Eastern Theater

CS sword belt plate.

Oval CS plate, Eastern Theater.

CS rectangular sword belt plate.

Oval CSA plate.

Pewter C.S.A. plate, Western Theater.

Oval CS plate, Western Theater.

CSA plate, Western Theater.

Oval CS plate.

BELT PLATES 143

Buttons

UNIFORM BUTTONS WORN by Confederate military personnel numbered in the millions and were very diverse. Pre-war southern militia and Federal issue buttons were very prominent. Civilian buttons of all types were used and enormous numbers of buttons imported from England and a lesser number from France saw use. Local Confederate and southern state production added to this number.

There were three-piece, two-piece buttons, and those that were solid cast with drilled shanks, all produced by manufacturers throughout the Confederacy. Material used was primarily die struck sheet brass and some had tin backs, while there were some cast pewter and turned wood buttons. A very

Staff officers' and officers' buttons (mostly English imports).

Enlisted men's coat and vest buttons.

Texas buttons.

North Carolina state seal buttons, including two with starburst variations.

few special orders were made of precious metals. The face of the button presented the letter of branch of service, a staff eagle or state seal or some variant of the seal.

English-manufactured buttons included all branches of army service as well as the Confederate States Navy. These buttons were imported by the gross on blockade-runners and substantial numbers were still available on original cards in the 1960s. Some dies still exist and many buttons have been restruck and others have been manufactured in England and elsewhere abroad in recent years. Fine collections of Southern buttons may be viewed at the Museum of the Confederacy, Richmond, Va.

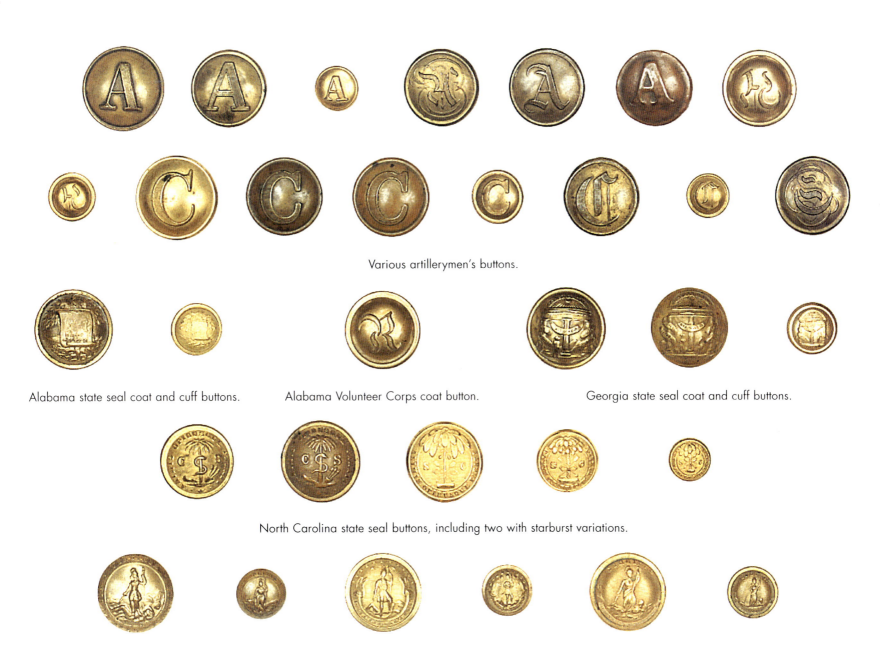

Various artillerymen's buttons.

Alabama state seal coat and cuff buttons.   Alabama Volunteer Corps coat button.   Georgia state seal coat and cuff buttons.

North Carolina state seal buttons, including two with starburst variations.

North Carolina state seal buttons, including two with starburst variations.

BUTTONS 145

RANK INSIGNIA AND DECORATIONS

THE CONFEDERATE FORCES adopted Army Regulations of 1861 that stipulated the manner of dress and rank designation. It is not surprising that the Confederate Regulations were similar. In many instances the "U.S." was changed to "C.S." in the text with no other alterations.

The new regulations specified different rank designations for wear on the collar, sleeve and forage cap somewhat like the style of the French army. Second lieutenants wore a single strip of gilt lace on each side of the collar. Two strips signified a first lieutenant and three a captain. Majors wore one star on the collar, lieutenant colonels two and full colonels three. All general officers wore three

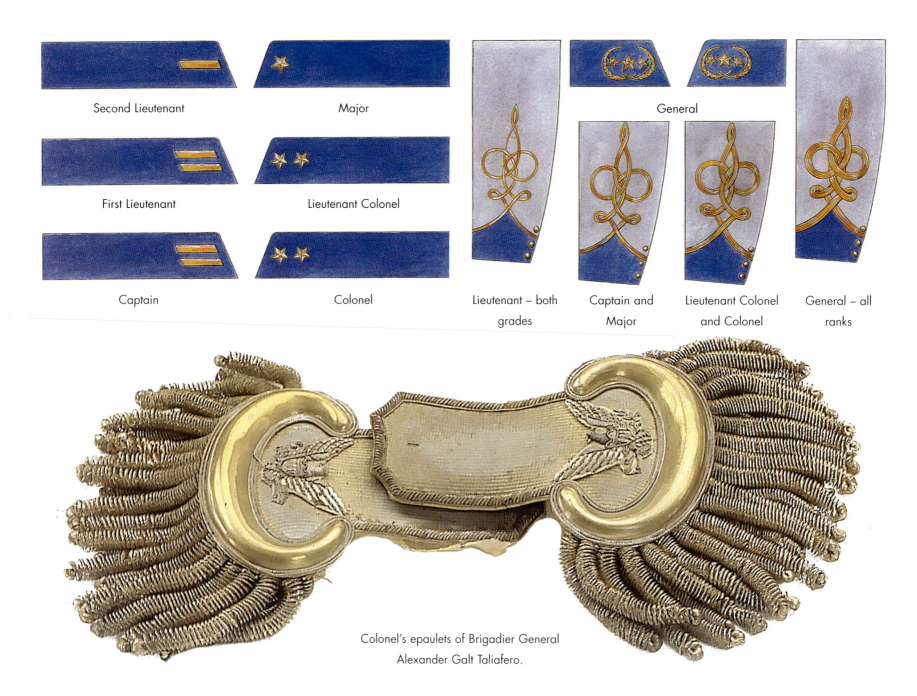

Colonel's epaulets of Brigadier General Alexander Galt Taliafero.

stars encircled by a wreath. On each sleeve were worn gilt cord galloons with each additional cord denoting higher rank. On the forage cap a quatrefoil on the top denoted rank based on the number of cords in it. Interestingly, many Federal officers in the chasseur units used galloons and quatrefoil.

Confederate units had no regulation insignia but there were a number of non-regulation state-associated symbols worn by the individual soldier. Louisiana soldiers wore some crescent-shaped pins and Texas and Mississippi troops wore star-shaped pins. Surviving examples appear to be jeweler-made with name and unit engraved on the pin.

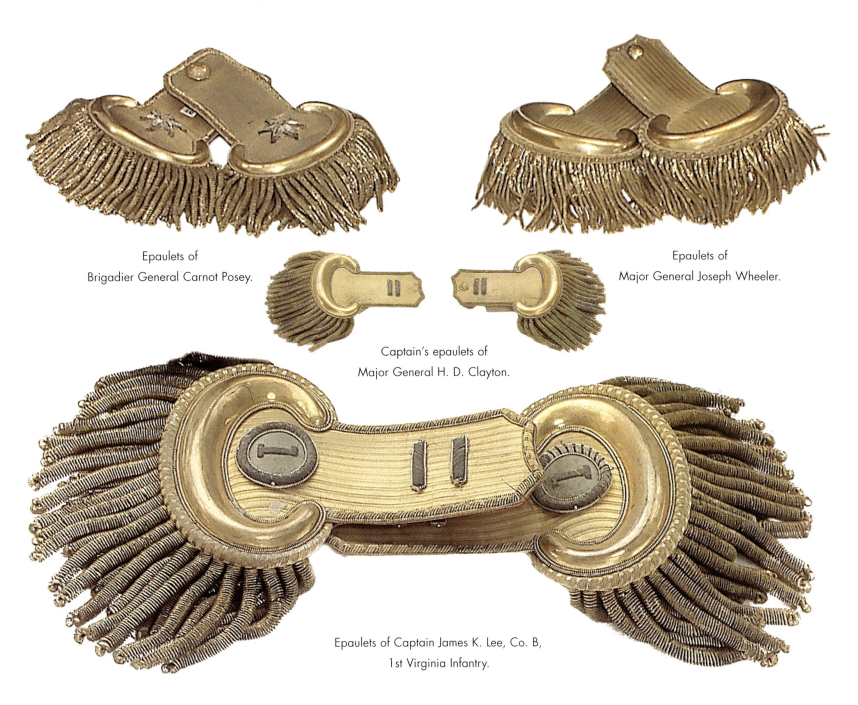

Epaulets of Brigadier General Carnot Posey.

Epaulets of Major General Joseph Wheeler.

Captain's epaulets of Major General H. D. Clayton.

Epaulets of Captain James K. Lee, Co. B, 1st Virginia Infantry.

Muskets, Rifles and Rifle-muskets

THE STORY OF longarm procurement in the Confederacy is very similar to that of revolvers and carbines. Without any existing native firearms industry to take the lead, the brand new Confederate Ordnance Department had to build from the ground up. There was no lack of enthusiastic and willing contractors who desperately wanted to fulfill government contracts for patriotism and personal gain but there was an enormous lack of experience and reality as concerns production techniques, and particularly mass-production.

The southern states were blessed because of arms distributed under the Militia Act of 1808, and southern agents had been tireless and active in buying whatever arms were available to them in the north. The northern manufacturers' desire for profit, even as the war began, enabled these Confederate agents to buy current production arms and ship them south.

There were over 296,000 arms seized at Federal arsenals and installations located in Augusta, Georgia, Baton Rouge, Louisiana, Charleston, South Carolina, Fayetteville, North Carolina, Little Rock, Arkansas, Mount Vernon, Alabama, Atlanta, Columbus, Macon, Oglethorpe and Savannah, Georgia, Montgomery, Morgan and Selma, Alabama, Columbia and Moultrie, South Carolina,

British Pattern 1853 Enfield rifle-musket, plus cartridge box.

Belgian Pattern 1842 short rifle.

British Pattern 1842 short rifle, plus saber bayonet and scabbard.

148 EQUIPMENT OF THE CONFEDERATE FORCES

Fayetteville rifle.

British Kerr's Patent rifle.

British Brunswick rifle, with bayonet.

MUSKETS, RIFLES AND RIFLE-MUSKETS 149

Muskets, Rifles and Rifle-Muskets

Memphis and Nashville, Tennessee, Jackson, Mississippi, San Antonio, Texas, and New Orleans, Louisiana. These arms were Model 1816 flintlock muskets, many altered to percussion, Hall's flintlock, breechloading rifles, Model 1841 rifles, Model 1842 muskets, Model 1855 rifle-muskets and rifles, and miscellaneous patterns. Only about 24,000 of these weapons were considered modern firearms. An immediate effort was made to alter to percussion those arms that still operated by flintlock, and this work was carried out at arsenals in Atlanta, Knoxville, Memphis, and Nashville, Tennessee, and Columbus, Mississippi.

The capture of the U.S. Arsenal at Harpers Ferry on April 19, 1861, was an incredible windfall.

British Whitworth Patent rifle, with telescopic sight.

British Pattern 1853 Enfield musketoon, with ramrod in stowed position.

J. P. Murray musketoon, with ramrod in stowed position.

150 EQUIPMENT OF THE CONFEDERATE FORCES

Besides the wagon loads of finished firearms and partially finished parts, the gun-making machinery seized there facilitated the manufacture of arms at Richmond and Fayetteville.

The Richmond Armory was the most successful and productive Confederate Ordnance facility during the war. Estimated production was just over 31,000 rifle-muskets and about 1,300 short rifles. In addition, the arsenal assembled over 1,200 Model 1842 muskets from parts and repaired nearly 25,000 arms. No other installation achieved anywhere near this success.

The rifle-making machinery went to the arsenal at Fayetteville, North Carolina, and arms delivery began in 1862. By the time the armory was finally destroyed by General Sherman's 3rd

Palmetto Armory Model 1842 smoothbore musket, with bayonet fixed and ramrod in stowed position.

C. Chapman musketoon, with ramrod.

Cook and Brother musketoon, with ramrod.

Dickson, Nelson and Company muzzle-loading rifle with ramrod in stowed position.

MUSKETS, RIFLES AND RIFLE-MUSKETS 151

Muskets, Rifles and Rifle-Muskets

Division, 14th Army Corps, on March 11, 1865, about 8,600 excellent brass-mounted, two-band .58 caliber rifles had been made there.

Cook and Brother had a private armory in New Orleans until Federal occupation, and then established another in Athens, Georgia. The Cooks produced rifles by August 1861, these being the first army rifles manufactured in Louisiana. Cook products were brass-mounted copies of the English Pattern 1856 short rifle and other derivative English arms. The factory ceased production around July-August 1864 because the government had failed to pay for work completed. Cook and Brother manufactured nearly 7,800 firearms. Some of these were carbines and musketoons, but the bulk of

Davis and Bozeman muzzle-loading rifle, with ramrod in stowed position.

Late design Fayetteville muzzle-loading rifle, with ramrod in stowed position.

Morse smoothbore muzzle-loading musket, with ramrod stowed and bayonet fixed.

Mendenhall, Jones and Gardner muzzle-loading rifle, with ramrod stowed, shoulder strap, and British Lancaster bayonet and scabbard.

them were short rifles. Their production was easily the highest of any of the private contractors.

A number of manufacturers tried to fill the needs of the Ordnance Department. Most furnished longarms based on the popular Model 1841 rifle, usually omitting the patch box to simplify production and lower the cost. Mendenhall, Jones & Gardner fabricated just over 2,500 rifles but many companies produced fewer than 500 rifles and most did not approach 1,000.

At the beginning of the war Chief of Ordnance Colonel Josiah Gorgas recognized the manufacturing limitations of his new country and sent agents to England and Europe to buy modern arms available there. Under the able stewardship of Caleb Huse and other agents, over 400,000

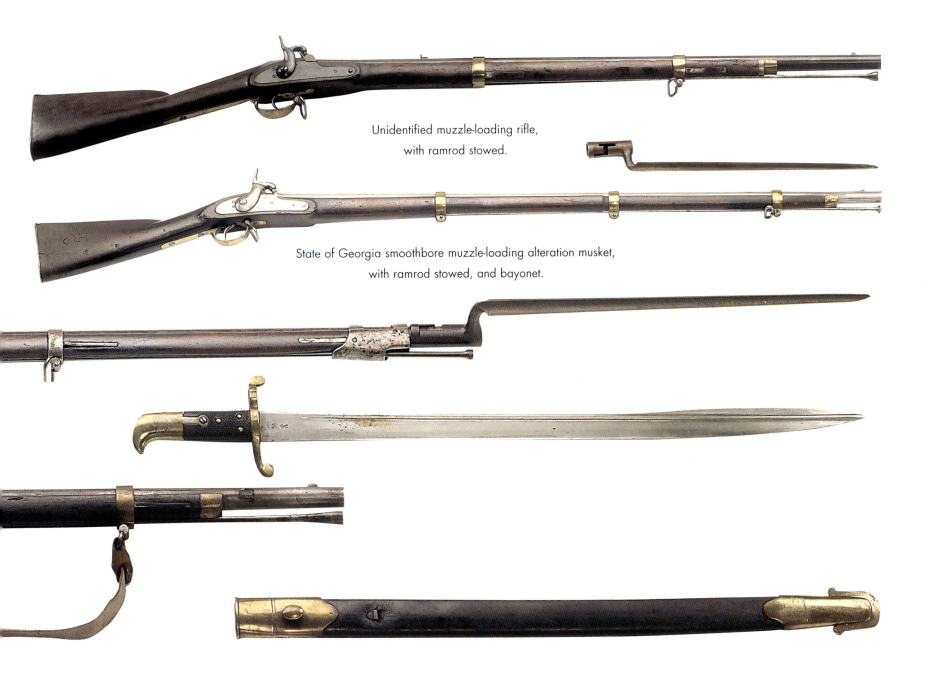

Unidentified muzzle-loading rifle, with ramrod stowed.

State of Georgia smoothbore muzzle-loading alteration musket, with ramrod stowed, and bayonet.

Muskets, Rifles and Rifle-Muskets

English Pattern 1853 rifle muskets and derivative arms were shipped to the Confederacy. The English arms industry was second only to captured Federal arms as a source of weapons for the Confederate army. In particular, Huse had great success in Austria where he purchased 100,000 Model 1854 Lorenz Rifles, which eventually made their way to the Army of Tennessee.

Somehow, despite all the problems faced, Confederate Ordnance managed to arm half a million men over a four-year period and keep them in the field. This could not have been done without the contributions of England and Austria to the Confederate war effort and the capture of so many Federal guns. Confederate-manufactured longarms probably made up less than 15 percent of the arms in the hands of the Southern soldiers.

J. P. Murray muzzle-loading rifle with ramrod stowed.

C. Chapman muzzle-loading rifle, with ramrod.

Pulaski muzzle-loading rifle, with ramrod in stowed position.

H. C. Lamb muzzle-loading rifle, with ramrod stowed.

Read and Watson late model muzzle-loading rifle, with ramrod stowed.

Cook and Brother muzzle-loading rifle, with ramrod stowed.

Late model Richmond muzzle-loading rifle-musket, with ramrod stowed, and cotton strap.

MUSKETS, RIFLES AND RIFLE-MUSKETS 155

CARBINES

The Richmond Armory was the major source of carbines for the Confederacy. However, estimated total production there was fewer than 5,500 carbines. S. C. Robinson of Richmond, and then the central government, made a copy of the Sharps Carbine and their total combined production was under 5,000.

Cook and Brother of New Orleans, later Athens, Georgia, manufactured about 1,500 carbines and G. W. Morse of the State Works in Greenville, South Carolina, fabricated fewer than 1,000.

All the other known carbine and musketoon manufacturers – Bilharz, Hall & Company, C.

Dickson, Nelson and Company cavalry carbine, with ramrod stowed.

J. P. Murray cavalry carbine, with ramrod.

British Terry's Pattern 1860 cavalry carbine, with breech mechanism open for loading.

British Pattern 1853 Enfield cavalry carbine, with ramrod stowed.

Tallahasee cavalry carbine, with ramrod stowed.

Tarpley cavalry carbine, with hammer cocked.

Le Mat cavalry carbine.

CARBINES

Chapman, Davis and Bozeman, Dickson, Nelson & Company, Kean, Walker & Company, J. P. Murray, Read and Watson, Tallassee Armory, and J. H. Tarpley – did not produce as many as 5,000 such weapons during the whole war. Total carbine and musketoon production in the Confederacy was fewer than 18,000.

English Pattern 1856 cavalry carbines and Pattern 1853 artillery musketoons run through the

S. C. Robinson Sharps cavalry carbine.

Morse cavalry carbine, with breech exposed for reloading.

Keen, Walker and Company cavalry carbine, with breech mechanism open for reloading.

Bilharz, Hall and Company rising-breech cavalry carbine, with breech open for reloading.

158 EQUIPMENT OF THE CONFEDERATE FORCES

blockade are estimated to have been fewer than 5,000 arms.

The majority of arms in the hands of Confederate mounted forces were those captured from Federal troops. The Confederate cavalry used Spencer, Sharps, Burnside, Smith and Gallagher carbines plus all the other Federal carbines then in use. A small number of shotguns were carried until replaced by a good breechloading Federal weapons.

Cook and Brother cavalry carbine, with ramrod stowed.

Bilharz, Hall and Company muzzle-loading cavalry carbine, with ramrod stowed.

Richmond cavalry carbine, with hammer cocked, ramrod stowed, and carrying strap.

Calisher and Terry cavalry carbine, with ramrod stowed, and leather strap. This firearm was owned by Major General J. E. B. Stuart.

Pistols and Revolvers

The Militia Act of 1808 provided for the periodic transfer of arms from the Federal government to the individual states. Many of these arms were obsolescent but some were current models then in use by the army. To supplement these arms some of the southern states sent agents to northern firearms manufacturers such as the Colt Patent Firearms Manufacturing Company, Hartford, Connecticut, and the Whitney Arms Company, New Haven, Connecticut, to purchase arms for the prewar state militia in 1860 and early 1861.

Confederate or state forces seized Federal installations within their respective borders at the beginning of the Civil War. These included a number of Federal arsenals within the southern states that contained sizeable numbers of arms of all types. It is with the arms thus received, seized and

Wilson & Leavitt Army revolver.

British Webley double action revolver, .44 caliber.

British Kerr .44 caliber revolver.

Colt Model 1848 Army revolver, 3rd Model.

French-manufactured pinfire revolver.

British Tranter single-trigger revolver.

purchased, that the Confederate forces marched off to war.

Among these arms were a number of single-shot flintlock and percussion pistols, Models 1836 and 1842, and some even earlier patterns. A few flintlocks were issued to eager volunteers, but every effort was made to alter obsolete flints to the percussion system. A number of southern contractors performed this work, among them Thomas J. Adams and S. C. Robinson of Richmond, Virginia. These single-shot .54 caliber pistols were inadequate at best when facing an adversary who was eventually armed with a breechloading carbine and a six-shot revolver.

Southern agents were relatively successful in securing Colt revolvers even after the beginning of the war. A number of Colt Model 1860 Army Revolvers with full fluted cylinders were sent south and

British Tranter double-trigger Navy revolver.

British Beaumont-Adams revolver, with belt and holster.

British Tranter double-trigger Army revolver.

Remington New Army revolver, with holster.

PISTOLS AND REVOLVERS 161

Pistols and Revolvers

Colt was corresponding with Confederate authorities as late as June 1861, weeks after the first shot was fired at Fort Sumter in April 1861.

Throughout the war the Confederate forces were forced to utilize any weapon that was available, which accounts for the incredible variety of types in service. Battlefield captures and post-battle cleanup by Confederate Ordnance personnel reaped great rewards. Thousands of modern revolvers were acquired in this manner, primarily current issue Colt Model 1851 and Model 1860 revolvers and Remington Old and New Model Navy and Army revolvers.

Handguns imported from abroad provided another source. Large numbers of small arms were imported from England, then one of the largest armament producers, but the U.S. Navy made

Model 1836 pistol alteration.

Leech and Rigdon revolver.

Griswood and Gunnison late model revolver.

Rigdon, Ansley revolver.

Spiller and Burr revolver.

strenuous efforts to prevent such warlike supplies reaching the South. About 9,000 English Kerr revolvers were imported, in addition to smaller numbers of Webley, Beaumont-Adams, and Tranter revolvers. Kerr revolvers were well liked by the soldiers lucky enough to be issued this weapon. Le Mat revolvers made in Belgium, France and then England totaled some 3,000 arms and French LeFaucheux pinfire revolvers were obtained in some numbers, although availability of ammunition was always a problem. Imported handguns equaled or exceeded revolver production within the Confederacy

The least productive source of small arms for the Confederacy was the local ordnance industry. Despite all the patriotic projections and government encouragement and funding, the fledgling

Virginia Manufactory 1st Model pistol alteration.

Virginia Manufactory 2nd Model flintlock pistol, with ramrod.

Palmetto Model 1842 pistol, with integral ramrod unstowed.

J. and F. Garret pistol, with integral ramrod stowed.

J. H. Dance and Brothers Army revolver.

Pistols and Revolvers

industry suffered from terminal lack of experience. None of the individuals or companies that secured government contracts had any prior experience in the manufacture of firearms. Confederate revolver manufacturing failed to achieve anywhere near projected production. One of the greatest problems of this business was the dependence on untrained and unskilled labor. Even with Ordnance Inspecting Officers overseeing production there was a lack of quality control and early rejection rates were high.

Most of the Confederate revolvers were patterned after the Colt Model 1851 Navy or the Whitney Navy revolver. Griswold and Gunnison of Griswoldville, Georgia, managed to produce about 3,700 brass-framed .36 caliber arms, while Spiller and Burr produced about 1,500 brass-framed .36 caliber revolvers based upon the Whitney pattern. Leech and Rigdon and Rigdon, Ansley & Company

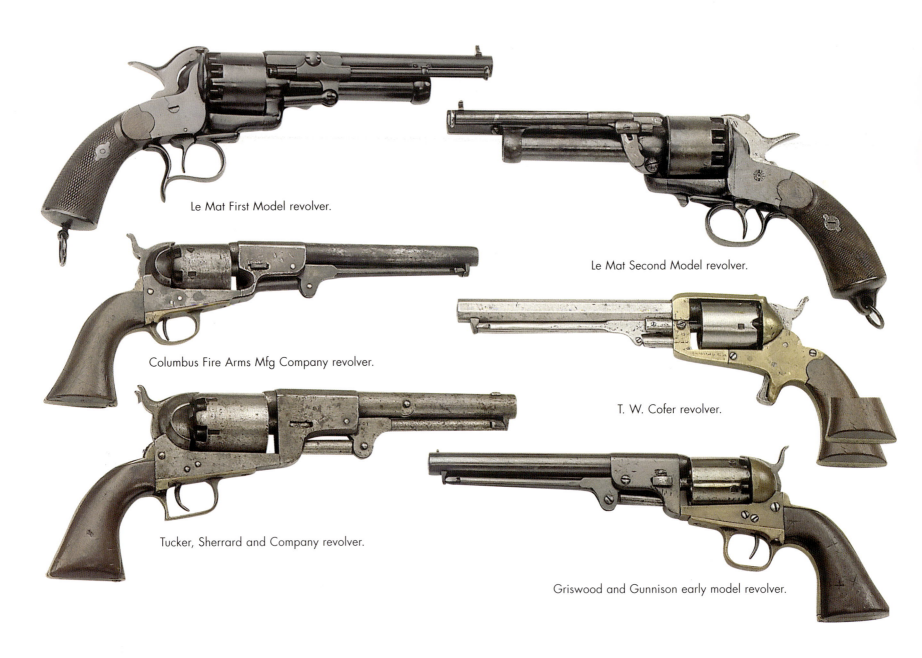

Le Mat First Model revolver.

Le Mat Second Model revolver.

Columbus Fire Arms Mfg Company revolver.

T. W. Cofer revolver.

Tucker, Sherrard and Company revolver.

Griswood and Gunnison early model revolver.

together produced another 3,000 revolvers. All the other makers, Augusta Machine Works, Cofer, Columbus Firearms Manufacturing Company and J. H. Dance & Brothers, made so few revolvers that the sum total was less than 10,000 revolvers produced and delivered during the war, and some of these were of dubious quality.

In the final analysis, there were far more Colt and Remington revolvers in the hands of the southern soldiers than the pitiful few Confederate revolvers manufactured. Very low survival rates have made these pistols extremely rare today. There have been more reproduction Confederate revolvers of various models fabricated in Italy since the Civil War Centennial, 1961-1965, than were ever made in the Confederacy during the Civil War.

British Adams Patent revolver, with box containing tools and tins of percussion caps.

Model 1842 flintlock type of percussion pistol (captured from Federals).

Clark, Sherrard and Company revolver.

Le Mat Second Model revolver in .41/65 caliber.

Le Mat revolver (with 18 gauge shotgun barrel under main barrel).

PISTOLS AND REVOLVERS 165

Cartridge and Cap Boxes

The cap box and cartridge box in Confederate service were direct copies of those in Federal service. Size and construction were similar but Confederate cartridge boxes rarely mounted a cartridge box plate. Confederate accouterments also showed ersatz substitutions, such as lead or wood buttons instead of brass, and weatherproof painted canvas instead of leather. The South had to use whichever materials it could lay its hand on.

Some boxes such as those made at the Baton Rouge Arsenal had brass buttons and the quality was commensurate with the finest Federal box. Painted canvas accouterments such as those made by Williams, Brands & Co. and N. Crown & Co of Columbus, Georgia, are excellent examples of ersatz in the Confederacy. A number of different style carbine boxes were made that conformed to no Federal pattern.

Boxes with "CS" or the manufacturer's name embossed on the flap are extremely rare today. The Confederate Navy had sets of CSN-embossed accouterments similar to those of its Federal counterpart. These boxes are extremely rare with only two types known to have been made. All Confederate accouterments saw hard use in service, and survival was limited. Thousands of sets of accouterments were imported from England for the Pattern 1853 longarms.

Cap boxes were a favorite souvenir of Federal soldiers, and a surprising number appeared in GAR museums in the North. Several of the rare embossed boxes have been reproduced and are available today.

Cap box for attachment to waist belt.

Standard cap box.

Cavalry carbine cartridge box.

Cartridge box and carrying strap.

Cavalry cartridge box complete with loops for attachment to waist belt.

Alternative style of cavalry carbine cartridge box.

166 EQUIPMENT OF THE CONFEDERATE FORCES

Militia cavalry cartridge box, with shoulder harness.

Cartridge box with embossed George state seal plate.

CS-embossed cap box.

Pouch for percussion caps.

CS-embossed cartridge box.

CS-embossed cap box.

CS-embossed cartridge box with carrying strap.

Cartridge box, cap box, and waist belt.

CARTRIDGE AND CAP BOXES 167

Tools and Accessories for Firearms

THE RICHMOND LABORATORY produced a broad spectrum of ammunition and fuzes. Cartridges were packaged ten to a paper-wrapped pack with a printed or stenciled label denoting caliber or, in the case of fuzes, length of time of fuzes. The cartridges were placed in the cartridge box, unopened packs in the bottom of the tin and loose cartridges in the top of the tin. The standard cartridge box held forty rounds. Fuzes and friction primers were carried in a gunner's fuze pouch on a waist belt and remained in the protective packs until ready for use.

Bullet molds were issued to troops in the field to enable the production of lead projectiles and use of loose powder in case the supply of fixed ammunition was exhausted. A considerable number of English .577 brass molds were in use throughout the war.

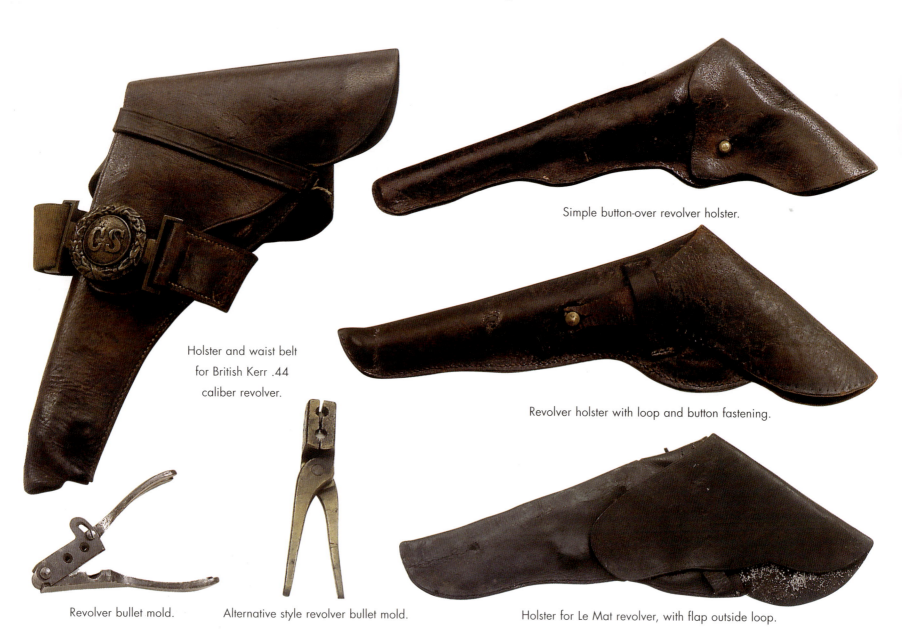

Holster and waist belt for British Kerr .44 caliber revolver.

Revolver bullet mold.

Alternative style revolver bullet mold.

Simple button-over revolver holster.

Revolver holster with loop and button fastening.

Holster for Le Mat revolver, with flap outside loop.

168 EQUIPMENT OF THE CONFEDERATE FORCES

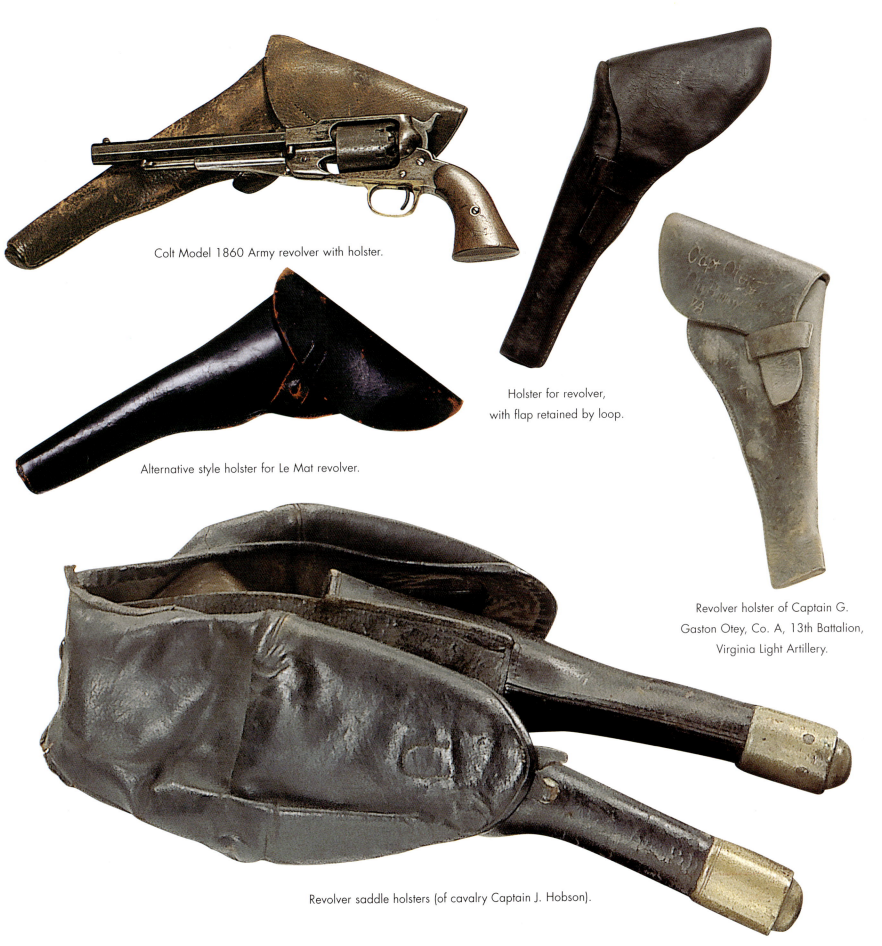

Colt Model 1860 Army revolver with holster.

Holster for revolver, with flap retained by loop.

Alternative style holster for Le Mat revolver.

Revolver holster of Captain G. Gaston Otey, Co. A, 13th Battalion, Virginia Light Artillery.

Revolver saddle holsters (of cavalry Captain J. Hobson).

TOOLS AND ACCESSORIES FOR FIREARMS

Edged Weapons

THE GREAT MAJORITY of edged weapons carried by Confederate soldiers were captured or seized Federal weapons. Many career officers who had prior army service carried their prewar service sword, including Generals Lee and Jackson. A significant number of English Pattern 1822 Foot Officers' swords, Pattern 1822 Cavalry Officers' sabers, and Pattern 1853 Troopers' sabers were imported through the blockade, as were an unknown number of Austrian sabers.

Edged weapons made within the Confederacy were mainly copies of U.S. patterns that in turn were copies of French patterns. Confederate edged weapons generally did not exhibit the quality of Federal counterparts. Most had sand cast hilts that were roughly finished in some cases, and forged blades that lacked a fine polish. Most enlisted men's sabers had sheet iron scabbards and some scabbards were even copper or wood.

Some of the officers' swords made by Thomas, Griswold and Company of New Orleans early in the war were as fine examples of the swordsmith's art as could be found. The sword of General Sterling Price is an excellent example. The same can be said of the sword presented to General Braxton Bragg made by Bissonnet of Mobile. A. H. Dufilho of New Orleans also made beautiful

Model 1840 cavalry saber in metal scabbard.

Unmarked cavalry saber with scabbard made of sheet copper.

Saber in the style of Nashville Plow Works, Nashville, Tennessee, featuring distinctive grip guard.

Unmarked cavalry saber with wooden scabbard.

Short sword and wooden scabbard as used by members of Confederate Foot Artillery.

Engineer officer's sword with brass-mounted metal scabbard, made by Boyle, Gamble and Company.

Leech and Rigdon staff and field officer's sword variant.

Cavalry officer's saber and scabbard, made by Thomas Griswold and Company.

EDGED WEAPONS 171

Edged Weapons

swords. Some products of Thomas Leech and Co., the Memphis Novelty Works, and Leech and Rigdon were exceptionally fine weapons. Most of these great swords were made before the end of 1862. The Confederate States Armory in Kenansville, North Carolina, The Nashville Plow Works and College Hill Arsenal, both in Nashville, Tennessee, and Louis Haiman and Brother in Columbus, Georgia, developed their own hilt design that featured the letters CS or CSA, and these were quite striking.

Boyle, Gamble and Company cavalry officer's saber and scabbard. The blade has no fuller (groove cut into the blade to lighten it).

Cavalry officer's saber and scabbard, made by W. J. McElroy.

Staff and field officer's saber and scabbard, made by Kraft, Goldsmith and Kraft.

College Hill foot officer's sword and scabbard, made in Nashville, Tennessee.

Considering the relatively small number of Confederate edged weapons fabricated during the war, a surprising number have survived. They were obviously popular war souvenirs for Federal soldiers. Since the early 1960s hundreds, possibly thousands of excellent reproductions of at least eighteen different pattern Confederate edged weapons have been made overseas and are available in the United States.

College Hill staff and field officer's sword and scabbard.

Louis Haiman and Brother foot officer's sword and scabbard.

Louis Haiman saber carried by Dawson Terrell Light Artillery.

Saber of Brigadier General Archibald Gracie, Jr., killed at Petersburg, 1864; made by Louis Haiman and Brother.

EDGED WEAPONS 173

Side Knives and Bayonets

ACCEPTING THE EVIDENCE of contemporary photographs, the large D-guard or side knife would appear to have been a favorite weapon of the Confederate soldier. In reality such weapons, after the fervor of patriotism died down, were replaced with small utilitarian knives or folding pocket knives. Some showed considerable skill in fabrication and others were no more than sharpened wagon springs or files with a wrought-iron D-shaped guard. Scabbards were usually leather, some with tin or brass mounts and some made entirely of tin.

The greatest source of bayonets was unquestionably battlefield captures and seizures of Federal models, and importation from England and Austria. Richmond Arsenal fabricated triangular, fluted steel socket bayonets and what was described in the ledgers as a 3-square bayonet whose triangular blade had no flutes and was flat on all three sides. These weapons had sockets with and without clasps. The Fayetteville Arsenal also made a socket bayonet and Heck, Brodie & Co, near Raleigh, North Carolina, produced 3-square bayonets. Fayetteville Arsenal in North Carolina and Cook and Brother at New Orleans and later Athens, Georgia, manufactured brass-hilted saber bayonets. Unidentified makers made others in small quantities.

Infantryman's side knives.

D-guard side knife with scabbard.

D-guard side knife with scabbard.

Officer's spear point side knife.

174 EQUIPMENT OF THE CONFEDERATE FORCES

Side knife and scabbard, made by W. J. McElroy.

Boyle, Gamble and MacFee "bowie" bayonet with scabbard.

Side knife made by Boyle, Gamble and Company, Richmond, Virginia.

Raleigh Bayonet Factory socket bayonet with scabbard.

Fayetteville saber bayonet.

Georgia Armory saber bayonet housed in scabbard.

SIDE KNIVES AND BAYONETS 175

Haversacks, Water Bottles and Canteens

HAVERSACKS CARRIED BY Confederate personnel were essentially non-standard, non-issue and made of leather or canvas in a variety of forms.

Confederate soldiers captured and liked Federal Model 1858 spheroid canteens because they were good equipment. Copies, as well as tin drum canteens in various sizes and configurations, were produced by the thousands. There were two patterns with "CS" embossed in the sides and one is thought to have been made in New Orleans. Several variant double-spout tin canteens were manufactured in very limited quantities. A significant quantity of English wood canteens was imported. The most common Confederate-made wood canteen was the Gardner, with turned wood sides and iron hoops, and a variation with brass hoops and strap loops existed. The Nuckolls Patent two-piece shaped wood canteen was a rare type and few survived.

Slightly worse for wear haversack for artilleryman, with different-shaped flap compared with haversack at left.

Artilleryman's haversack, with carrying strap.   Wooden canteen.   Officer's haversack.

176 EQUIPMENT OF THE CONFEDERATE FORCES

British pattern water bottle (canteen).

Fabric-covered canteen with stopper and carrying strap.

Fabric-covered tin drum canteen.

Wooden canteen carried by artillery officer.

Fabric-covered canteen carried by artillery officer.

Wooden canteen carried by artillery officer.

Ringed body metal canteen.

Tin drum canteen.

HAVERSACKS, WATER BOTTLES AND CANTEENS 177

MUSICIANS' INSTRUMENTS AND EQUIPMENT

THE CONFEDERATES ADOPTED Federal regulations on musicians. Each regiment was allowed a band of sixteen privates. In combat they were on the firing line or served as hospital orderlies and surgeons' assistants. Each company was assigned two field musicians, a fifer and drummer, for infantry and a bugler for cavalry and artillery. These communicated the orders of the day, just as in the Federal army.

The bands used the same type of brass wind instruments, all of which were made in the northern instrument centers prior to the war. Drums were made in Richmond, Virginia, by the Confederate Drum Manufactory operated by James Wright; the related Richmond firm of Wright and Bell also made drums. Extant examples are standard snare drums of the same approximate size as a Federal drum.

Clarinet used by Confederate Army band.

Three different styles of fifes.

Small horn insignia as worn by some musicians.

RIGHT: Members of the regimental band of the 26th North Carolina, photographed at Salem, N.C., during the period 1862-1863. Their instruments would have been made in the North prior to the war.

Snare drums with drum sticks; the drum on left has a carry strap.

Alternative styles of bugles, the one at lower right has attachment points for a carry strap.

MUSICIANS' INSTRUMENTS AND EQUIPMENT 179

NATIONAL, UNIT AND BATTLE FLAGS

THE CONFEDERATE BATTLE FLAG is one of the most easily recognizable symbols in the world today. It has had a mystique about it since inception that is impossible to explain. Well over a century after the war ended the Battle Flag continues to be the center of controversy.

It was just one of many flags used by Confederate forces during the war and was never the National Flag. The first pattern National Flag, the "Stars and Bars," was adopted at the beginning of the war. It bore a startling similarity to the Federal "Stars and Stripes" and caused such confusion that

Battle flag of the 6th Kentucky Infantry, displaying its battle honors.

180 EQUIPMENT OF THE CONFEDERATE FORCES

The Confederate First National Flag carried by the "Dixie Rangers."

Flag of the Florida Independent Blues, Company B, 3rd Regiment Florida Volunteer Infantry.

NATIONAL, UNIT AND BATTLE FLAGS

a new pattern was adopted in May 1863 utilizing the battle flag as a canton with a white fly known as the "Stainless Banner." It unfortunately was mistaken as a flag of truce if there was no breeze to extend the fly so another change was authorized in March 1865 that placed a red bar on the end of the white fly. The war ended the next month and very few of this pattern were produced.

The Battle Flag was actually a design submitted as a national flag by William Porcher Miles but not accepted. It was enthusiastically adopted as the Battle Flag at the urging of General P. G. T. Beauregard. The Quartermaster Department ordered 120 flags for the Army of Northern Virginia to be made of dress silk and these were issued at the end of 1861. With silk exhausted, wool bunting was

Virginia state seal flag, unit unknown, proudly boasting *Sic Semper Tyrannis* ("Ever Thus to Tyrants") beneath the figure of "Liberty."

South Carolina state seal flag of Co. B, 5th Regiment, South Carolina Volunteer Infantry.

Flag of 7th Regiment Virginia Volunteer Infantry, which was part of Kemper's Brigade of Pickett's Division during the Battle of Gettysburg.

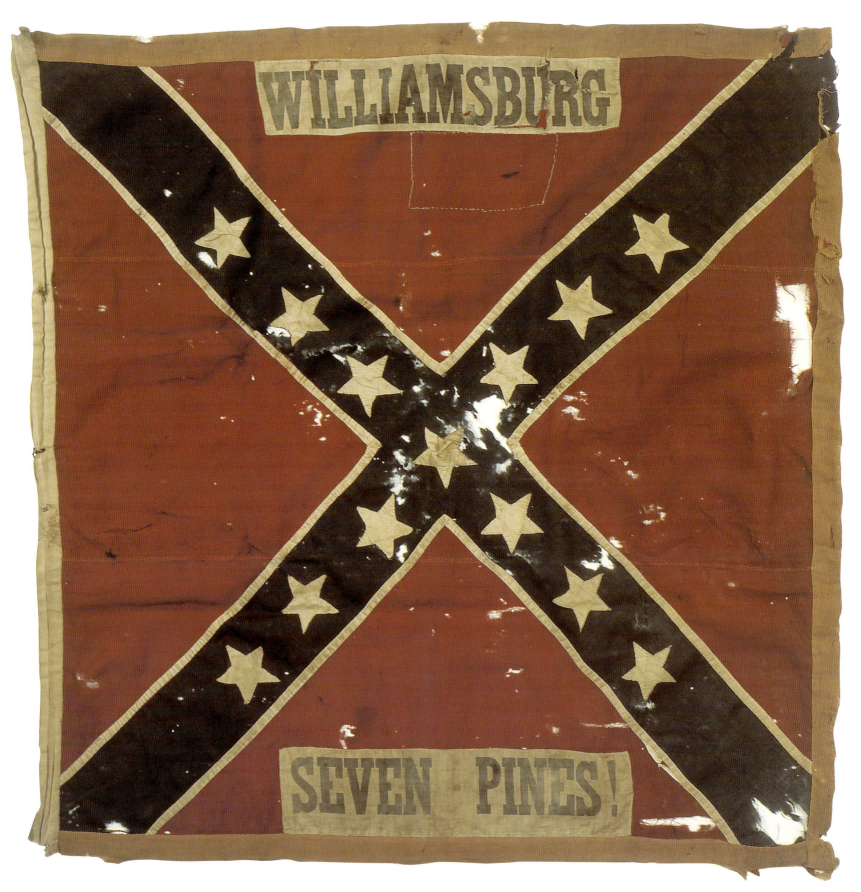

Believed to be the flag of the North Carolina Infantry Regiment (second bunting issue), captured by Federal troops at the Battle of Chancellorsville.

NATIONAL, UNIT AND BATTLE FLAGS 183

National, Unit and Battle Flags

Flag of Courtney's Virginia High Constabulary (third bunting issue), captured at Spotsylvania Court House, May 1864.

Flag of 8th Regiment Virginia Volunteer Infantry, presented to the unit by General P. G. T. Beauregard in recognition of the valor displayed by its members at the Battle of Balls Bluff (Leesburg), Virginia, October 21, 1861.

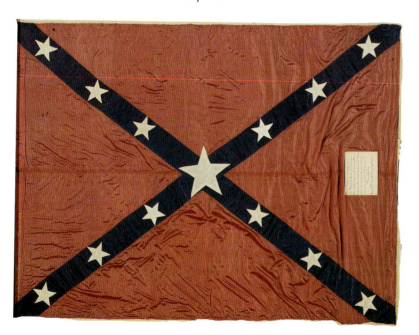

Flag of Van Dorn Guards of Texas. Two units are known to have carried this name: Company A, 8th Regiment Texas Volunteer Infantry; and 4th Battalion, Texas Artillery. Note the large central star.

National flag, second pattern variant, of the 9th Regiment, Arkansas Volunteer Infantry, carried in engagements throughout the Western Theater.

substituted. Vast quantities were captured at the U.S. Navy Yard in Norfolk, Virginia, and more was imported from England. The Richmond Clothing Depot became a major supplier of flags on a regular basis and seven variant bunting issues were produced by the end of the war. The Staunton and Charleston Clothing Depots also produced variant patterns. The War Department approved the addition of battle honors to flags in July 1862 although the practice was already widely adopted in the field. Eventually, private contractors added battle honors and the Richmond Quartermaster Depot placed battle honors on flags in subsequent issues.

Flags were the chief means of recognition on the 19th century battlefield. The War Department never approved the Battle Flag nor authorized its use by the different armies in the field. Flag patterns were left to the discretion of the army commanders. In the western armies this resulted in multiple

Flag of the 9th Regiment Virginia Volunteer Infantry.

Hardee Pattern flag of an unknown regiment, Army of Tennessee, captured at Lookout Mountain, Battle of Chickamauga, November 24, 1863.

Flag of 1st Kentucky Brigade, Army of the Tennessee – known as the "Orphan Brigade," consisting for most of the war of the 2nd, 4th, 5th, 6th and 9th Kentucky Infantry Regiments, together with a unit of artillery.

NATIONAL, UNIT AND BATTLE FLAGS **185**

National, Unit and Battle Flags

patterns, with eight designs carried by the Army of Tennessee in 1863. General John Bell Hood officially ordered the western forces to adopt a rectangular version of the Battle Flag that was issued in January 1864 to replace all the Hardee, Polk and other patterns in use. His efforts were not successful and uniformity was never achieved.

Confederate flags were square, rectangular, swallowtail or pennant shaped and made of silk, wool or cotton bunting and broadcloth by quartermaster facilities, ladies aid societies, nuns and patriotic sewing circles. Thus it should be no surprise that so many variations exist.

Flag of 57th Regiment Georgia Volunteer Infantry, at one time a unit of General Bragg's corps, Army of Mississippi/Army of Tennessee. The shape of the large pink border around the flag, and the twelve six-pointed stars, indicate that this is the second pattern flag of Bragg's corps. The first had been smaller and squarer.

Polk Pattern unit flag, possibly of the 16th Tennessee Infantry. General Leonidas Polk's battle flag featured the cross of St. George, which was also the emblem of the Episcopal Church of which Polk was Bishop of Louisiana.

Unit flag of 7th Regiment Mississippi Volunteer Infantry, at one time a unit of Hindman's Division, A. S. Johnston's Army of Tennessee, issued to the regiment after March 1864.

Flag of 1st and 3rd (combined) Regiments Florida Volunteer Infantry, issued to the unit in 1864.

NATIONAL, UNIT AND BATTLE FLAGS **187**

The Battles

By William C. Davis

ABOVE: Pattern 1851 artillery enlisted man's stamped brass insignia, worn on the hat.

LEFT: This is believed to be the first actual photograph of the U.S. Army in combat. Showing evidence of camera shake, it was made, under enemy artillery fire, by Mathew Brady, at the Battle of Fredericksburg, Virginia, in 1863.

THE BATTLES: INTRODUCTION

WHEN NORTH WENT to war with the South, an avalanche of armies were loosed that almost crushed the continent beneath their weight. Before they were done, this still-rural land would soak up the blood of more than 2,000 battles of varying size (some say even 10,000), from tiny skirmishes between a few dozen men, such as Jones' Hay Station, to battles like Gettysburg of 200,000 and more, the biggest conflicts ever seen in this half of the globe.

Most of those battles were unknown even at the time, and quickly forgotten by all but those who fought in them. Even more melted into the shadows of history as the old veterans and their generation died away. But a few, an epochal few, remained, and remain still, so traumatic that they cannot be escaped; so symbolic that they will not be forgotten. Almost a century and a half after the fact, the world's generals – the great and the would-be – still study Stonewall Jackson at Chancellorsville. Ending his days after being one of the great military commanders of all time, Dwight D. Eisenhower chose to live amid the fields and monuments of Gettysburg. No American can ever forget that even D-Day in 1944 did not spill as much American blood as the single day at Antietam in 1862.

The Civil War was the most tragic of all wars, one between father and son, friend and friend,

BELOW: The reality of war: a grim view of a Union cemetery at City Point, Virginia, where some of the soldiers who had fallen or who had succumbed to sickness were laid to rest, with unmarked headstones for those who could not be identified.

literally setting brother against brother. It was the American Iliad and Odyssey, a New World War and Peace – not just spots on the map, but places in the heart.

No one expected either the trauma or the blood, much less the battlefields, when it all started to unfold. After all, there had been decades of talk and more talk, with always some blustering and posturing, some threatening and then some compromising. It may never have left everyone satisfied entirely, but at least it left them with some alternative to violence in their minds and hearts. Even when 1860 brought the final collapse, when the election of Abraham Lincoln left the slave states feeling so threatened that secession and the resultant challenge to the Constitution seemed to be the only recourse, most still hoped for a peaceful resolution. When state after state voted to withdraw from the Union, hopeful – some said naïve – Southerners expected to be allowed to go in peace. When departed states banded together to form the new Confederate States of America in February 1861, they felt confident that their united front would be their defense and that the North would have to treat them as independent. Even when local militia groups answered drum and trumpet calls to muster on the village greens, and when those companies joined others to form regiments and started concentrating at Washington and Richmond and other cities to form small armies, still many said there would be no war. The boastful spoke of drinking all the blood shed in any conflict to come out of secession, so confident were they.

When Lincoln took power he made it clear from the first that his oath to preserve the Constitution left him no choice but to restore the Union and Federal authority in all of the states. Still he wanted to talk, however, to stall, to delay, always in the hope that time would calm rising passions. Yet even before he took power, there was already a festering sore that could not be relieved. For all of the Federal property seized without resistance or violence throughout the seceded states, there were a few spots where men in Federal blue still held on. Fort Monroe, Virginia, and Fort Pickens, Florida; both were secure in Union hands, with no fear of violent seizure. As for the Confederates, these places, while an irritant, did not pose a real challenge.

But there was another, right in the center of Charleston Harbor, South Carolina, a slap in the face to the Confederacy right under the eyes of the people of the city called the seedbed of secession: Fort Sumter. Only a few score Yankees, in an unfinished fortress, with guns not yet entirely mounted, living in unfinished barracks, sat there in their blue like a splinter beneath a nail, a painful irritant that would not go away and that could not be ignored. Finally, abandoning negotiation that could never have yielded a satisfactory solution for either side in any case, the Confederates acted. On April 12, 1861, they turned Fort Sumter into the first battleground of the Civil War.

Early in the pre-dawn hours a series of last-minute negotiations passed back and forth between General P. G. T. Beauregard's massed emissaries and the Federals in the fort. Attempts to force a capitulation or evacuation short of the hostilities came to nothing, however, and at 4:30 a.m. a signal

The Battles: Introduction

shell from a James Island battery became the first shot of the Civil War. At once a ring of flame erupted around Charleston Harbor as battery after battery opened fire. For some time the Federals held their fire, then began a desultory answering fire from their few working guns. When the Yankees did shoot back, the Confederates cheered, not wanting their victory to be too easy. But soon Sumter's wooden barracks were blazing, and though not a man was harmed, Major Robert Anderson, in command of the garrison, decided to yield when he saw no hope of being reinforced.

As such, it was not much of a battle nor much of a field. Sumter could have been taken by a corporal's guard sooner or later, by starvation if by no other means. As for the site, it was not land or field at all, but a mountain of brick and mortar erected on an artificial island of rubble, most of it, ironically, granite from New England brought to the South.

But it was enough to start the war. Within hours of the surrender of the Sumter garrison on April 13, the war drums beat North and South. From towns great and small the regiments marched forth. Washington for a time found itself cut off from the rest of the North, with Virginians facing it across the Potomac and rebellious Marylanders at its back. When relief regiments marched through Baltimore to get to the capital, a riot claimed lives, and the first blood. Then, with Washington relieved and Maryland and its rebellious citizens more or less subdued, the Yankees began to put their feelers out south of the Potomac. There were skirmishes then. Men began dying in combat. Then in June came what they called a battle at Big Bethel, though by later standards it would be little more than a minor encounter, and soon forgotten.

But all the while, the armies kept growing. A time would come, soon enough, when they would meet, not just a few hundred to a side, but in their tens of thousands, to decide issues far greater than Baltimore or Big Bethel or even Fort Sumter could settle. More than 2,000, or maybe even 10,000, battlefields awaited their making, and among them waited places that were to become immortal. They already had their names. They needed only the unfolding of events. The earth and the blood were waiting to meet.

And a terrible meeting it was, too. By war's end, a little more than four years after the Confederate guns first roared against Fort Sumter, over six hundred thousand had died, most killed by disease, but still a quarter million as a result of wounds. More than one million wounds had been inflicted. A whole generation of maimed and crippled men were left to live out their days however they could. A section of the country had been ravaged of all its resources, material, agricultural, and human. An angry scar had been slashed across the landscape and the soul of its people, a scar that could never be erased. Four million Americans, once enslaved, were now free, with little but their freedom and the clothes on their backs.

An old question about the nature of the Union and the relation of the states to the Federal government had been settled at last. The old Union was gone forever, washed away in a flood of

BELOW: A Federal sentry and a companion sit among the rubble of what is left of Richmond's industrial buildings. Much of what was not leveled by the Federals was destroyed by the Confederates to make the manufacturing plants useless to their enemies.

blood and tears, but faith still remained in many to create a new America. And most of all there remained the nagging question. Had it all, or any of it, been worth the price? Within weeks of Lee's surrender, Union soldiers met on the old Manassas battlefield, where the first full-scale but still rather haphazard fight had taken place those years before, to dedicate one of the very first monuments to commemorate the dead and what they died for. It was only the first of thousands of such ceremonies, to be repeated on every great battlefield of the Civil War, a continuum that, together with the reenactments of many of the battles, still endures to this day. And always when they come to the bloodied land, now peaceful beneath the sod that covers the dead and their sacrifice, always they wonder. Had it all been worth the cost?

First Manassas (First Bull Run), July 21, 1861

THE LEADERS

UNION
Department of Northern Virginia:
Brigadier General
Irwin McDowell

CONFEDERACY
Army of the Potomac:
Brigadier General
Joseph E. Johnston
Brigadier General
Pierre G. T. Beauregard

SIGNIFICANT UNITS

UNION
13th, 69th and 79th New York
2nd Wisconsin
Rickett's Battery I,
1st U.S. Artillery

CONFEDERACY
Hampton Legion and
4th South Carolina
2nd, 4th, 5th, 7th, 11th, 24th,
and 27th Virginia
13th Mississippi

NO ONE HAD ever expected the lovely countryside between Washington and Richmond to play host to warring armies. Moving out from Centreville, at upper right, Brig. Gen. Irvin McDowell's leading column under Major General David Hunter moved along the Warrenton Turnpike until turning off in a wide sweep upstream to cross Bull Run at Sudley Ford, being followed by Samuel P. Heintzelman. Meanwhile Brig. Gen. Daniel Tyler was to move straight along the turnpike to the Stone Bridge. Gen. P. G. T. Beauregard, who was chiefly responsible for the Confederate dispositions, was taken much by surprise. Having expected an attack on his right, he had put the bulk of his forces in place to cover the lower fords, while his left at the Stone Bridge had nothing more than the half-brigade of Brig. Gen. Nathan Evans to cover it.

McDowell's plan worked wonderfully at first. Tyler did his job well, and Hunter crossed at Sudley without opposition. When the first Federal masses swept down from the ford, Evans was hard-pressed to hold them at Matthews' Hill, but hold them he did, even after Heintzelman's division started to come on the field. Meanwhile the Rebel high command reacted quickly and started sending reinforcements to the endangered left flank. Brig. Gen. Bernard Bee arrived, then Col. Francis Bartow and his Second Brigade, and the Confederates delivered a stunning counterattack. Still, Yankee

BELOW LEFT: Shells fired from both sides leveled the house of the Henry family early on July 21, 1861, during the first significant battle of the war. Mrs. Henry was carried to what was thought to be a place of safety but was brought back to the house before the battle ended, and died from wounds caused by a shell fragment.

pressure forced them back from Matthews' Hill and across Young's Branch, toward Henry Hill. Now Gen. Thomas Jackson arrived, to become a "stone wall", and even more reinforcements finally stabilized the line, though charge and countercharge continued for two hours or more.

Steadily the lines grew longer, extending to the southwest as more and more units reached the scene. Tyler finally started to cross at the bridge and a ford just upstream, while the fight for Henry Hill became ever more desperate. Then accidents gave the battle to the Confederates. Maj. Gen. Oliver O. Howard's Yankee brigade came into line at the far Federal right and went into attack, just as new Rebel troops arrived at the right place and time to hit him in the flank. His brigade melted, and then when more Confederate regiments emerged on this crumbling Union flank, and Jeb Stuart's cavalry delivered a demoralizing charge, the Federal right simply fell apart, spreading panic all along the line. Running for their lives, the bluecoats raced back across the bridge and Sudley Ford, for Centreville, and eventually Washington.

McDowell lost 2,900 out of about 20,000 engaged; the Confederates 2,000 out of about 17,000 engaged. As well as the men, the North lost cannon and supplies, and the morale boost this first battle would have given them.

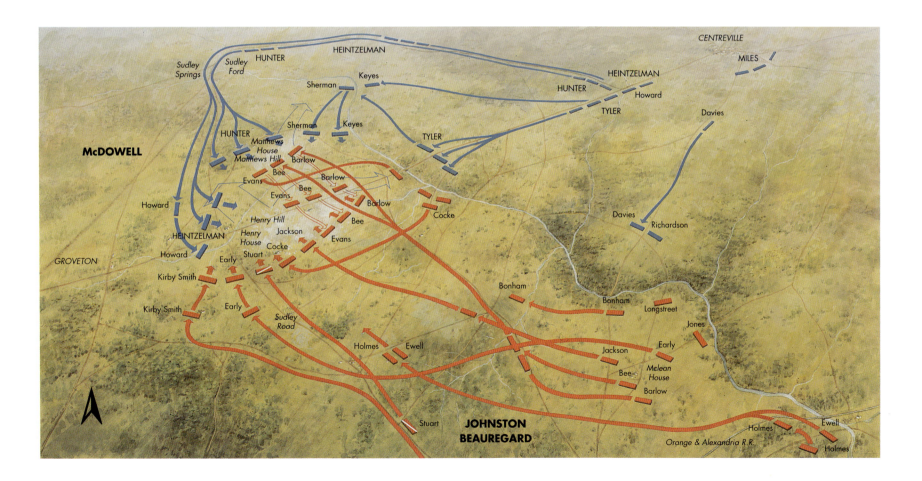

Sergeant, 79th New York Infantry ("Highlanders"), 1860-61.

First Lieutenant, 2nd Rhode Island Infantry.

FAR LEFT: Sergeant, 79th New York Infantry, the "Highlanders," 1860-61, which modeled itself and uniform on the British Army's 79th Cameron Highlanders, initially formed in 1859 of four companies of entirely Scots immigrants. In full dress, the men wore kilts, a doublet, sporran, hose, garters and silver-buckled shoes. In the field, however, they wore light blue trousers (as they did at First Manassas) or Cameron tartan pants, dark blue blouses, and regulation kepi.

LEFT: First Lieutenant, 2nd Rhode Island Infantry, in distinctive early war uniform of the state's first 90-days regiments: pleated blouse with full skirt and rolled collar. His revolver is the Colt New Model Army, .44 caliber; his sword a Model 1850 foot officer's sword.

RIGHT: At First Manassas, the 1st Virginia Cavalry regiment, formed by J. E. B. Stuart into a regiment from independent companies, achieved renown as the "Black Horse Cavalry," the origin being obscure. They wore chiefly homespun clothing of plain gray or butternut, with black facings on light-gray short jackets and trousers. Broad-brimmed black hats with plumes completed their attire.

Trooper, 1st Virginia Cavalry Regiment, CSA, 1861-62.

Battle of Shiloh, April 6-7, 1862

The Leaders

Union
Army of the Tennessee:
Major General Ulysses S. Grant
Army of the Ohio:
Major General Don Carlos Buell

Confederacy
Army of the Mississippi:
General Albert Sidney Johnston
General Pierre G. T. Beauregard

Significant Units

Union
9th and 12th Illinois
81st Ohio
13th and 14th Missouri (Birge's Sharpshooters)
21st and 25th Missouri
12th Michigan
16th Wisconsin
Hickenlooper's 5th Independent Battery, Ohio Light Artillery
77th Pennsylvania
29th and 30th Indiana
34th Illinois

Confederacy
1st Arkansas
4th, 12th, and 19th Louisiana
15th and 22nd Mississippi
19th, 20th, 28th, and 45th Tennessee
154 Senior Tennessee
Rutledge's Battery A, Tennessee Light Artillery

Ironically, the Battle of Shiloh on a map looks far more organized and orderly than it did on the ground, where even units as small as a company had trouble staying together.

The advance of Gen. Albert Sydney Johnston and his four corps is seen at upper left. But very soon after the first elements struck Brig. Gen William T. Sherman's camps, their organization dissolved as brigades intermingled. Still, despite good resistance, the Federals were forced back. While Grant frantically tried to organize his surprised army, the Confederates pressed on until they came to Maj. Gen. Benjamin Prentiss and his command in and around the peach orchard at left center. Here the brave Prentiss and his men stopped the Rebel advance cold, and held it up for precious hours at what would ever after be called the Hornets' Nest. The fighting here became so severe, and the bluecoats so stubborn, that Johnston committed his Reserve Corps early in the battle, and then himself took a mortal wound leading a Tennessee regiment into the fight.

Meanwhile, Sherman frantically tried to hold the Federal right against renewed attacks, while the Rebel pressure on Prentiss continued. At last the Hornets' Nest had to fall, and with it the Union left flank collapsed. The Federals had no choice but to fall back all along their shaky line, contracting their lines yet again as they took position under the cover of the batteries that Grant massed on the bluff

BELOW LEFT: The Battle of Shiloh took place only a few days before this photograph was taken in April 1862, within a few hundred yards of this landing on the Tennessee River. General Grant's headquarters boat, the *Tigress*, is tied up second from right. Grant used the river, striking as it did through the heartland of Tennessee and north Alabama, to begin cutting the Confederacy in two, and it was command of the river with boats like these, bringing fresh troops and supplies, that made it all possible.

above the Tennessee River. Meanwhile, Maj. Gen. Lew Wallace finally began to approach from the far right, and Maj. Gen. Don Carlos Buell's marching divisions sped down from the north, at bottom right. The closing Confederates actually got within sight of the Tennessee, having pushed the Federals until their backs were to the river. But now Beauregard took command, and lost his determination, calling off the advance just as victory was seemingly within grasp.

Only now did the Federals' situation begin to improve. The night of April 8-7 saw the bombardment of Rebel positions by Federal gunboats, as well as the arrival of substantial reinforcements under the command of Buell and Lew Wallace (bottom of the map and far right). Having ferried his men across the river, Buell launched an attack on the morning of the 7th, taking the already exhausted Confederate troops by surprise. The battle was now renewed in earnest, as the Confederates tried to hold on to their positions in the face of increasingly successful assaults by fresh Union troops. By mid-afternoon, Beauregard ordered the withdrawal back towards Corinth, detailing Gen. John C. Breckinridge to cover the retreat.

The toll was terrible. Grant lost 13,000 out of his 40,000 engaged, and 10,700 out of 44,000 Rebels fell.

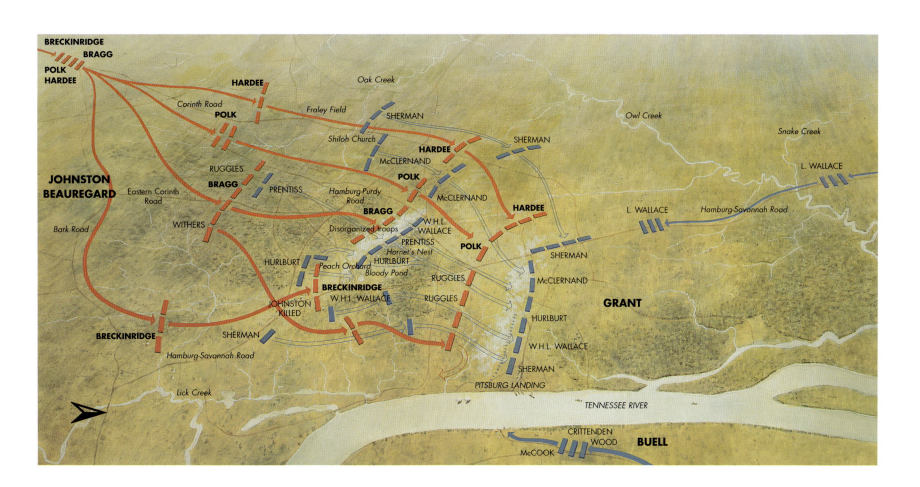

Foot soldier, Army of the Tennessee, U.S.A.

Private, 4th Kentucky Infantry, C.S.A.

FAR LEFT: The uniform of this Federal foot soldier in the Army of the Tennessee is similar to that of his Eastern comrades in the Army of the Potomac except for his battered wide-brimmed hat, instead of kepi.

LEFT: Little Johnny Clem may well have acted bravely in the battle, but sentimentality and legend turned him into "the drummer boy of Shiloh."

BELOW LEFT: The 4th Kentucky Infantry, part of the famed "Orphan Brigade," were considered the best soldiers in the Confederacy's Army of Tennessee. This private's all-cotton uniform includes the distinctive short jacket. His blanket was probably a quilt made by his mother. Late in 1864, the depleted units were turned into mounted troops, and they finished the war as cavalry.

RIGHT: This Confederate captain of Rutledge's 1st Tennessee Light Artillery, wears both collar insignia and shoulder straps indicating badges of his rank, in Federal style; similarly, his cuff facings are different from prescribed design, and the broad-brimmed hat in place of the customary kepi is also unusual in an artillery officer.

Captain, Rutledge's 1st Tennessee Light Artillery, C.S.A.

BATTLE OF SHILOH 201

THE SEVEN DAYS' BATTLES, JUNE 25-JULY 1, 1862

THE LEADERS

UNION
Army of the Potomac:
Major General
George Brinton McClellan

CONFEDERACY
General Robert E. Lee

SIGNIFICANT UNITS

UNION
1st U.S. (Berdan's) Sharpshooters
1st U.S. Artillery,
5th U.S. Cavalry,
2nd Delaware
1st, 9th, and 22nd Massachusetts
2nd New Hampshire
5th, 16th, 33rd, and 61st
New York
3rd Pennsylvania Cavalry
26th, 49th, 63rd, 69th, and
95th Pennsylvania
5th Vermont

CONFEDERACY
3rd, 5th, 11th, 15th, and
26th Alabama
7th, 8th, 15th, 18th, 21st, and
44th Georgia
1st Maryland (Confederate)
1st, 18th, and
20th North Carolina
1st South Carolina
Hampton's Legion,
4th Texas
2nd, 5th, 15th, 47th, 55th, and
60th Virginia

FEW CAMPAIGNS PRODUCING major battles saw as many fights, over as much ground, as the Peninsular Campaign of 1862, and particularly The Seven Days'. It began at Fair Oaks, or Seven Pines, a few miles west of Richmond, at right center. The battle was not well managed by either side, and its only positive result was the elimination of Gen. Joseph E, Johnston and the emergence of Robert E. Lee.

Lee struck first at Beaver Dam Creek at the extreme right Unfortunately, circumstances, including a tardy Stonewall Jackson, prevented Lee's plans from working. Undaunted, he pressed on, striking again at Gaines' Mill on June 27, at lower extreme right. Here Lee scored a definite victory, but still missed a chance to make it decisive. Thus he pushed on, and once again had a chance to catch the Yankees split in two at Savage's Station on June 29, at lower right center. Yet once again a crushing victory eluded him as Jackson once more failed in his vital part of the plan. Lee's frustration at not being able to get his army to work in the field the way it could on his maps began to tell on him, yet he held onto the offensive nevertheless.

The next day he struck again at Glendale, at left lower center. With his divisions set to come at McClellan from three directions at once, Lee hoped for the decisive victory that had eluded him for the past several days. But again execution did not equal planning, and McClellan slipped the trap to

BELOW LEFT: One of Major General George B. McClellan's hundred or more regiments in the Army of the Potomac on parade at Cumberland Landing on the Virginia Peninsula in May 1862. The men were being prepared for the "Young Napoleon's" push that he planned would take the army "on to Richmond," the Confederate capital. But a formidable foe emerged to thwart him: Robert E. Lee drove McClellan back and saved the capital against seemingly overwhelming odds.

take position on Malvern Hill about two miles further south, and almost overlooking the horseshoe shaped bend of the James River at left.

Unfortunately, by now Lee was at a loss, worn out by campaigning, frustrated in every plan. In desperation, he resorted to a massive frontal assault against McClellan's positions, thinking them battered by his artillery. But the Yankees mowed down his weary Rebels with dreadful cost, and McClellan withdrew the next day, unharrassed. However, the prestige of Northern arms and that of McClellan himself had taken a serious blow, while in contrast the Confederacy had discovered in Robert E. Lee a general in whom it could fully place its trust and loyalty.

Holding onto his small piece of the Confederacy, McClellan and his largely undefeated army sat out the coming months, with his prestige in the North seriously damaged and the confidence of Lincoln severely shaken. McClellan refused to budge and, despite orders from Washington, maintained vociferously that the proper line of advance should be through the Peninsula. This would have great bearing on the outcome the Battle of Second Manassas (Second Bull Run), which was fought August 29-30, 1862. The campaign cost him more than 10,000 of nearly 100,000 in his army. Lee suffered nearly 20,000 out of his 80,000.

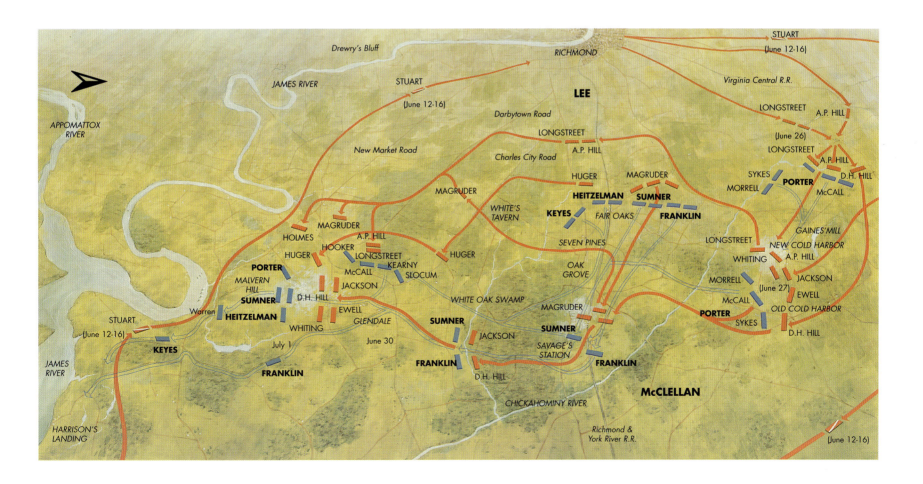

Second Lieutenant, 5th New York Infantry, U.S.A.

Sergeant, 6th Pennsylvania Cavalry ("Rush's Lancers"), U.S.A.

FAR LEFT: The 5th New York Infantry, also known as Duryee's Zouaves, was one of the more colorful of the Union regiments. This 2nd Lieutenant's bright red kepi and trousers differing distinctly from regulation. In battle, the red pants made standout targets for Confederate sharpshooters.

LEFT: Originally uniformed and equipped like any other cavalry regiment in the army, the 6th Pennsylvania – called "Rush's Lancers" after its colonel, Richard Rush – later adopted to fight with a nine-foot lance, quite useless against the poorest rebel firearm, and soon discarded.

RIGHT: The 1st South Carolina Rifles was raised in 1861 by prominent politician James L. Orr. Their distinctive garb included matching coat and trousers of Confederate gray, trimmed with black at the cuffs and front seam and hem, with a black stripe running down the trouser legs, and vertical stripe running up from the cuffs to show rank of officers like this lieutenant.

FAR RIGHT: This 44th Georgia lieutenant colonel has a standard gray pattern uniform piped in black. He wears a two-piece Georgia state belt plate, and stars on his collar cut from brass sheet.

204 THE BATTLES

Lieutenant, Orr's Regiment, 1st Carolina Rifles, C.S.A. | Lieutenant Colonel, 44th Georgia Infantry, C.S.A.

Battle of Antietam (Sharpsburg), September 16-17, 1862

THE LEADERS

UNION
Army of the Potomac:
Major General
George Brinton McClellan

CONFEDERACY
General Robert E. Lee

SIGNIFICANT UNITS

UNION
7th, 51st, 57th, 61st, and
64th New York
5th New Hampshire
51st, 81st, and 106th
Pennsylvania
2nd and 6th Wisconsin
2nd U.S. Sharpshooters
Knap's Battery

CONFEDERACY
16th and 18th Mississippi
1st and 4th Texas
5th, 27th, 48th North Carolina
2nd and 20th Georgia
15th and 17th Virginia
8th, 10th and 13th Georgia

ROBERT E. LEE'S GREAT daring almost got him into fatal trouble when his invasion of the North, and his splitting of his army in the face of McClellan, found him with only half his command in Maryland, with his back almost literally to the Potomac. McClellan uncharacteristically opened the battle with an offensive, but soon abandoned almost any direct control of the fighting, leaving it to his corps commanders on the field. The fighting started when Gen. Joseph Hooker's corps at extreme right center, and Gen. Joseph Mansfield just below him, crossed the creek and pushed forward into the North Wood, the East Woods, and finally the terrible Cornfield.

The Yankees pushed forward to the Dunker Church before determined Rebels pushed them back. Meanwhile the II Corps under Maj. Gen. Edwin V. Sumner crossed the creek from bottom right center and rushed across the fields until it encountered Maj. Gen. Daniel Harvey Hill's determined but desperately outnumbered Confederates in the Sunken Road. Here the fighting raged like a tornado, sucking every available unit into it for hours.

At the other end of the lines, where Lee had depleted his forces to reinforce his left, McClellan gave the enemy valuable time by doing nothing. Not until late morning did Gen. Ambrose Burnside start trying to get across the creek, and then instead of looking to find the fording places available, he

BELOW LEFT: The war is over for these unidentified Confederate souls who have fallen near Dunker Church, Antietam, the scene of the bloodiest day in American military history. The bodies would probably have been left where they lay, stripped of useful weaponry and equipment. Mathew Brady brought home to people in the East the horrors of war when he held an exhibition of "The Dead of Antietam" in his elegant New York photographic studio.

persisted in sending his men across the Rohrbach Bridge. Here, at left center, Burnside squandered his men, brigade after brigade, while Isaac P. Rodman managed to get his people across at Snavely's Ford less than a mile downstream, and virtually unopposed. As a result, it was late afternoon before Burnside finally got across. Even then he was moving well toward Sharpsburg and Lee's rear, reaching the outskirts of the village when Lt. Gen. Ambrose Powell Hill providentially arrived at the last moment from Harpers Ferry and hit the Federals a devastating counterblow that stopped Burnside.

Hill saved the Army of Northern Virginia from almost certain destruction. Reacting quickly to his fortuitous delivery, Lee rushed reinforcements – especially artillery – into the line and succeeded in pushing Burnside back almost as far as the Rohrbach Bridge. There the battle ended at nightful, with both sides exhausted and unable to continue the slaughter. Lee, however, refused to use the cover of night to make sure of his escape and held the field for another day in defiance of McClellan. Here he stayed moving wounded and supplies until the night of the 18th-19th when his battered army finally made its way out of Maryland.

On the bloodiest day of the war, and indeed in all American history, Lee lost more than 10,000 casualties out of his 50,000, while McClellan suffered over 12,400 from his 85,000.

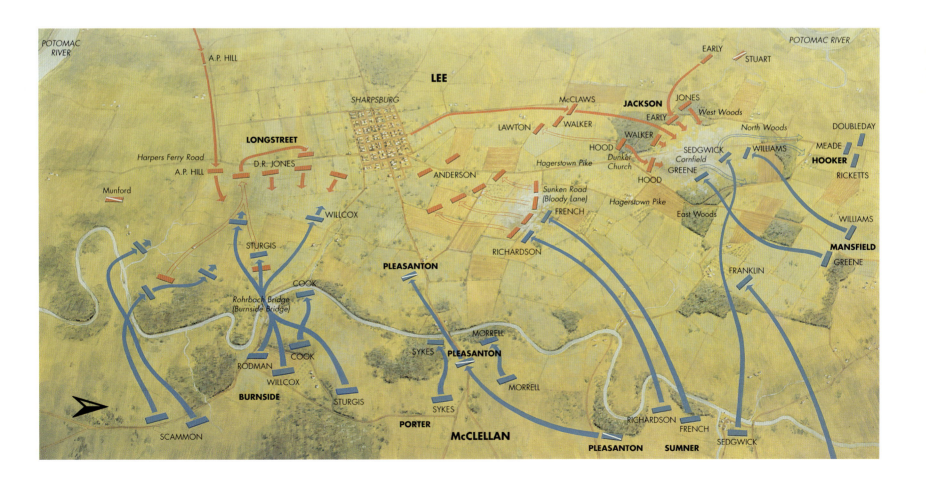

BATTLE OF ANTIETAM (SHARPSBURG) 207

Private, 9th New York Infantry Regiment ("Hawkins' Zouaves"), U.S.A.

First Lieutenant 9th New York Infantry Regiment, U.S.A.

FAR LEFT: In 1861 Rush C. Hawkins, veteran of the Mexican War, formed a new regiment, the 9th New York Infantry Regiment, starting with members of the old prewar Company of New York Zouaves. They were quickly dubbed "Hawkins' Zouaves" and wore skullcap, short jacket and baggy pants tucked into white leggings.

LEFT: Most Zouave units of the Union Army uniformed their officers in fairly standard dress, although this first lieutenant of the 9th New York Infantry belongs to one of the most colorful regiments. There was some confusion on the battlefield, because Zouaves of both sides shared many similarities, including the blue color of their jackets and the use of shoulder straps by officers.

RIGHT: The 11th Mississippi Infantry presented one of the handsome variations on the standard gray uniform of the Confederacy. The regiment was made up chiefly of prewar volunteer companies, many of which wore different garb. Most eventually wore slight variations of the state militia dress, the mid-thigh length gray blouse with red collar and red frogging on the breast, and red cuffs and trouser stripes. Headgear was predominantly the Hardee-style hat worn by this enlisted private, pinned up on right or left side, according to taste of the wearer.

Private, 11th Mississippi Infantry, C.S.A.

BATTLE OF ANTIETAM (SHARPSBURG) 209

Battle of Fredericksburg, December 13, 1862

THE LEADERS

UNION
Army of the Potomac:
Major General
Ambrose Everett Burnside

CONFEDERACY
General Robert E. Lee

SIGNIFICANT UNITS

UNION
7th Michigan
19th and 20th Massachusetts
89th New York
7th West Virginia
14th Indiana
24th and 28th New Jersey
4th and 8th Ohio
130th Pennsylvania
1st Delaware

CONFEDERACY
13th, 17th, 18th and
21st Mississippi
2nd, 3rd, 7th, 8th
and 15th South Carolina
16th, 18th and 24th Georgia
Cobb's Legion
Phillip's Legion
Washington Artillery

IN THE SPRING of 1862, Lee visited Fredericksburg, on the Rappahannock River, with President Davis and pronounced the position indefensible. But by December observation and circumstances had changed his mind. For the Federals, Burnside planned to cross the river, attack the town, and move on to Richmond, the Confederate capital, believing this would be the key to winning the war, and quickly.

When the Federal attack on the town came, it could not have played into Lee's hands more if he had planned it himself. Burnside put his hapless bridge-builders to work early on the first morning trying to "throw" their pontoon bridges across the Rappahannock right in front of Fredericksburg. Only daring and ingenuity got the job done, but it took all day. Downstream the bridges went across without great difficulty and Gen. William B. Franklin began crossing his brigades. Alas for the Federals, no one pressed anything that day, and Lee managed to position Lt. Gen. James Longstreet on his left behind the city, and Jackson on his right, in position for the attack expected for the morrow.

On December 13, Franklin sent Gen. George G. Meade and his division forward. The fighting became furious and prolonged, but by mid-afternoon had accomplished nothing, and Franklin did not press it further. The battle on the Confederate right was all but over.

In front of Fredericksburg itself, the Federals had massed all night in the streets of the city.

BELOW LEFT: Union officers examine damage to Confederate equipment caused by Federal gunners of the 2nd Massachusetts Heavy Artillery who had hurled 30-pound shells onto the battlefield of Fredericksburg. However, Lee's 6,000 men behind a stone wall had repulsed 40,000 Union soldiers. Torn between the elation of victory and horror at the human suffering, he said, "It is well that war is so terrible. Otherwise we should grow too fond of it."

Finally at noon portions of the II Corps started to move out of the outskirts and up the long gradual slope towards Marye's Heights. They were met by a wall of flame, yet on they went. When Rebel fire stopped them, more Yankees took their place, all of them striving toward the stone wall along the sunken road. Division after division went up the slope, only to be chewed by lead and spat back down again. Not one bluecoat ever reached the wall, yet the attacks went on almost until nightfall mercifully put the battle to an end. His foolishness had cost Burnside 12,653 casualties out of his magnificent army, more than 120,000-strong. Lee, by contrast, lost just 5,377 of the nearly 90,000 in his command. The armies remained in place, and Burnside had another division pinned down on the ground in front of the wall, without attacking. They had been sent there under cover of darkness to launch an attack at dawn, but found themselves as exposed as the dead and dying comrades who surrounded them on every side. The next day Burnside abandoned the field.

The Army of the Potomac would not abandon the town of Fredericksburg. Burnside at least wanted to hold on to some ground on the Rebel side of the river. For two days he remained in the town. Then at last he asked the Confederates on the heights for a truce to collect his casualties. This done, he retired back across the Rappahannock.

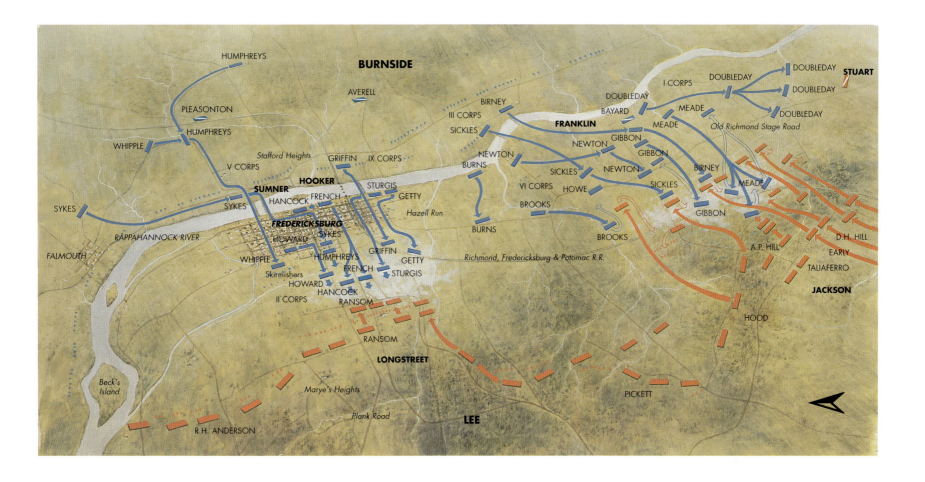

BATTLE OF FREDERICKSBURG

Gunners, Washington Artillery, C.S.A.

LEFT: The Washington Artillery of New Orleans was among the oldest and proudest of the private or fraternal artillery companies. Their uniforms and equipment evolved as the war progressed. Originally they wore dark blue frock coats or short artillery jackets with scarlet collars and cuffs over light blue trousers with scarlet stripes denoting the artillery arm. They wore scarlet kepis with blue bands and gold trim. Once in regular service they adopted gray uniforms, but retained their caps.

RIGHT: Early in the war the 2nd New Hampshire Volunteer Infantry actually went to war with the outmoded, Revolutionary-era swallow-tail coat with red trim and facings, gray trousers, the usual black leather accouterments and an almost ludicrous "coal scuttle" cap. Their distinctive "NHSM" belt plate, standing for New Hampshire State Militia, was almost the only element of their attire that was orthodox.

FAR RIGHT: This Confederate captain wears the regulation gray frock coat, trousers, and forage cap specified for his regiment, Co. G, 11th Virginia Infantry. The black trim on his trouser seams and cuffs and collar differs from the blue used on many other Virginia regimental uniforms. Unusual features are the brass shoulder scales with bullion epaulets.

Private, 2nd New Hampshire Volunteer Infantry, U.S.A.

Captain, Co. G, 11th Virginia Infantry (Lynchburg Home Guard), C.S.A.

BATTLE OF STONES RIVER (MURFREESBORO), DECEMBER 31, 1862

THE LEADERS

UNION
Army of the Cumberland:
Major General
William Starke Rosecrans

CONFEDERACY
Army of Tennessee
General Braxton Bragg

SIGNIFICANT UNITS

UNION
21st and 74th Ohio
37th Illinois
78th Pennsylvania
22nd and 42nd Illinois
42nd and 88th Indiana
3rd Ohio
15th Kentucky
1st Illinois Light Battery

CONFEDERACY
24th, 27th, 29th and
30th Mississippi
9th Texas
154th Senior Tennessee
8th, 16th, 38th, 51st and
84th Tennessee
Carnes' Tennessee Battery
5th and 8th Mississippi
13th, 16th and 20th Louisiana
5th Company Washington
Artillery

THE BATTLE OF Stones River, like several major engagements of the war, displayed the irony of both commanding generals conceiving the same battle plan. Both Generals Braxton Bragg and William S. Rosecrans planned a major movement against their opponent's right flank. Bragg struck first. Early on the morning of December 31 he launched Maj. Gen. John P. McCown's division against Maj. Gen. Alexander McCook's Federal flank, in a savage assault that swept the defenders back steadily. It was to be a "rolling" attack, each Rebel division in turn going in on the right of its predecessor. Gen. Patrick Cleburne went next, then Gen. Bernjamin Franklin Cheatham. As the morning progressed, almost the entire corps of Lt. Gen. William J. Hardee became engaged.

The Federals under McCook tried their best, but the foe caught them unawares, in unprepared positions, and never gave up the advantage. The whole Yankee right flank gave way in time, being pushed back nearly two miles, almost to the Nashville Pike. Had Bragg managed to sieze that road, the enemy line of retreat would have been cut off, and Rosecrans severely endangered.

In the end, however, a determined stand by Maj. Gen. Philip H. Sheridan anchored the failing Federal right, providing a pivot which at least retained more or less cohesive lines.

Meanwhile, on the other end of the field, elements of Maj. Gen. Thomas L. Crittenden's corps

had crossed Stones River, posing a seeming threat to Bragg's own right. Thus, Gen. John C. Breckinridge's division remained there to cover that flank through all of the morning. But Crittenden made no move against him, and by afternoon Bragg began calling for the Kentuckian's brigades on the west side of the river.

In the center of the lines, Bragg had launched a series of spirited, but uncoordinated attacks against an area called the Round Forest. Combined with the failure of the Federal right, the Round Forest attacks gained good ground, chewing up several Rebel brigades in the process thanks to Lt. Gen. Leonidis Polk's inept handling. Once Breckinridge's leading brigades arrived they, too, were sent into the wasteful assaults, and though they finally achieved some ground, still Rosecrans' center, though bettered, held on to their positions.

By the end of the day, the Union army had been severely mauled and Bragg wired to Richmond that he had a victory. But there was still fight in these bluecoats, and Bragg himself had suffered heavy casualties. That first day's fight ended at dusk, with exhausted Confederate soldiers falling back from the Federal line, unable to press home any more attacks. Both sides had taken a beating, neither was willing to quit the field while the other remained.

BELOW LEFT: After a fight exacting terrible losses on his command, Maj. Gen. Philip H. Sheridan finally brought a halt to the seemingly irresistible Confederate juggernaut at Stones River, providing an anchor for Rosecrans' ravaged forces on the Federal right.

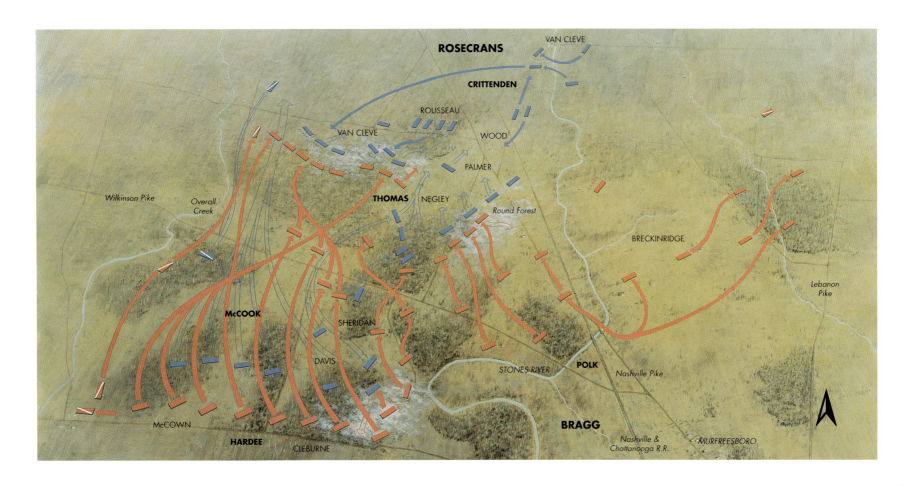

BATTLE OF STONES RIVER (MURFREESBORO) 215

Battle of Stones River (Murfreesboro), January 2, 1863

On January 1 the armies stayed relatively quiet, each side waiting for the other to make the next move. Bragg reorganized his battered center and left, and established a solid line to hold the ground taken the day before. Rosecrans evened his newly contracted lines, reformed his disorganized divisions on his right, and prepared to hold his ground. More than this, he anticipated that the enemy, having crushed his right, might next attempt to do the same on his left. As a result, he had Crittenden heavily reinforce his hold on the west bank of Stones River, bolstering it with a massive emplacement of more than forty artillery pieces.

Bragg wasted the morning of January 2, 1863, unfortunately failing even to perform adequate reconnaissance. He believed, however, that Rosecrans's right was now too well placed and reinforced to allow a successful renewal of the attack toward the Nashville Pike. Instead, he planned to send Breckinridge and his entire division in an attack against Crittenden – Breckinridge's childhood playmate. If successful, it could push the Yankees back and take the Nashville Pike from the north, leaving Rosecrans virtually surrounded.

But when Breckinridge got his orders, he argued vehemently that it was suicidal, that those guns of Crittenden's would destroy his command. But Bragg remained adamant, so much so that one of

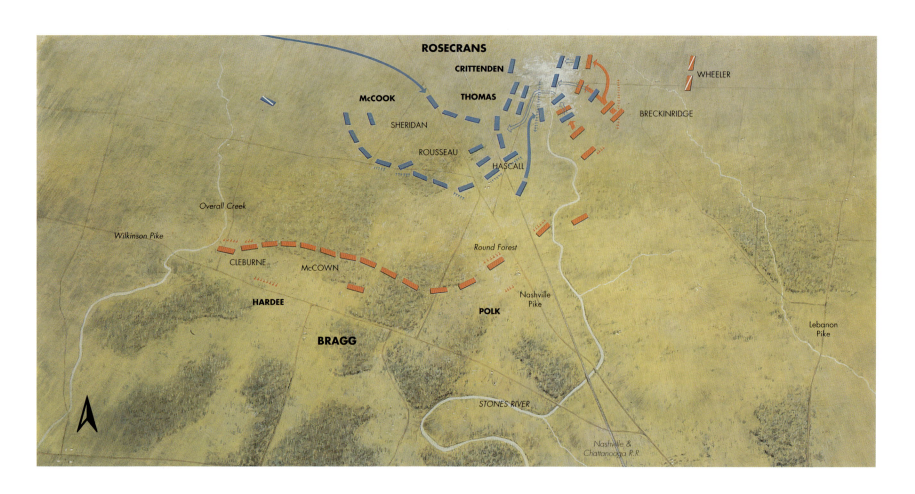

Breckinridge's brigadiers wanted to shoot the commanding general

Breckinridge sent his division forward at about 4:00 p.m., in a driving downpour of sleet and freezing rain. Initially the Confederates were successful, driving some advance units of Crittenden's back across Stones River. But then what Breckinridge feared happened. His men found themselves in an exposed position, and made it the worse when they pursued the fleeing Federals down to the river and themselves started to wade across. The massed artillery on the heights on the other side opened up on them with a dreadful barrage that mortally wounded one general and sent the attackers reeling back with 1,500 casualties. Crittenden did not follow up the repulse, and there the battle ended. Rosecrans lost 13,000 out of his 60,000-man army, greater losses than Bragg's 10,000 from his 50,000 Confederates. And for all of that, neither side truly gained a decisive advantage. Rosecrans held the field, and Bragg, having held the advantage all through December 31, had retreated his army south to the Duck River, there to set up another line of defense. Strategically the Federals now held the initiative, and the senior officers of the Army of Tennessee could spend the winter warring with their own commander, which would have repercussions far outlasting the military impact of the bloody winter days along Stones River.

RIGHT: Fighting from high ground, with the assistance of massed artillery, Maj. Gen. Thomas L. Crittenden helped his leader Rosecrans record a narrow but morale-boosting victory over the Confederates at Stones River. Crittenden was one of those Federal soldiers who had a brother (George) serving with the Rebels.

FAR RIGHT: Gen. John C. Breckinridge was ordered by Bragg to attack overwhelmingly superior massed Federal forces, including Crittenden's artillery on the high ground. It was madness: of just over 5,000 men who commenced the advance, fewer than 3,500 came back. Some of Breckinridge's officers were close to mutiny prior to the attack; those who survived could never forgive Bragg.

8th Texas Cavalry ("Terry's Texas Rangers"), C.S.A.

LEFT: One of the toughest mounted outfits in the South was made up of the rugged plainsmen of Texas, who went into battle with their distinctive "Wigfall" flag, named for a leading Texas politician, Louis T. Wigfall. Neither of these horsemen is shown carrying a saber, indicating the disdain that most cavalrymen had for that weapon. The sergeant has a rare Dance revolver, a Confederate-made copy of the Colt .44 Dragoon. The men are shown traveling light on Hope saddles, and the one in the background wears a lone star on his hat, symbolizing Texas.

RIGHT: General Braxton Bragg, the irascible, unstable general who sowed the seeds of dissension and mistrust in his own army, and right on the eve of a major battle, Stones River, that could settle Tennessee's fate. He was a man who, by temperament, saw enemies everywhere and, given his personality and character, he might have been right. In the aftermath of the battle, his generals, including Breckinridge, Hardee, and Polk, literally went to war with him over his conduct of the fight; this was a "war" fought in headquarters tents, newspapers, and the corridors of the South's War Department, and it undoubtedly played a part in the Confederacy's military downfall.

Battle of Chancellorsville, May 1-4, 1863

THE LEADERS

UNION
Army of the Potomac:
Major General Joseph Hooker

Confederacy
Army of Northern Virginia
General Robert E. Lee

SIGNIFICANT UNITS

UNION
41st, 45th, 54th New York
27th Indiana
53rd, 114th, 116th,
140th Pennsylvania

CONFEDERACY
4th, 12th, 21st, 44th Georgia
3rd, 5th, 6th, 26th Alabama
18th North Carolina

LEE HAD A remarkable facility for taking campaigns that started out badly against him and turning them into victories. He did it at Fredericksburg and here, on nearby ground five months later, he did it yet again, and more spectacularly.

Gen. Joseph ("Fighting Joe") Hooker's crossing of the Rapidan took Lee somewhat unawares. After passing Ely's and United States Fords, Hooker's legions advanced into the Wilderness. He had intended for Gen. John Sedgwick, facing Fredericksburg, to make a demonstration to hold the bulk of Lee's forces there, while Hooker moved against Lee's rear via the Orange Turnpike. Unfortunately, Sedgwick failed to act with his usual alacrity, allowing Lee to detach substantial portions of his army to advance to meet Hooker's threat.

On May 1, little fighting occurred as Hooker took Chancellorsville and tentatively pushed beyond. But Hooker was already losing his resolve, and now Lee seized a chance to take the battle away from him. He sent Jackson with several divisions on a wide sweeping flank march via the Brock Road, to reach the turnpike in Maj. Gen Oliver O. Howard's flank and rear. Shortly after 5:00 p.m., May 2, Jackson was in place and drove like lightning into the Federals. He sent Howard reeling back in shock and demoralization. Only darkness and disorganization stopped Jackson's advance.

BELOW LEFT: The dead and debris close to the stone wall and sunken road in front of Marye's Heights, near Fredericksburg, testify to the fury of the Confederate defense during the Battle of Chancellorsville in early May 1863. This photograph was taken by Captain A. J. Russell only hours after the Confederates withdrew. The battle ended as another victory for the South, but at terrible cost.

Hooker found himself in deep trouble. All the next day he struggled to hold his position at Chancellorsville, and even gained back a little ground. But just as Meade was ready to launch a very promising attack on Stuart's own exposed left flank, Hooker called off further offensive operations. Now he was concerned only to get his army out of this place intact.

The scene of action shifted to Fredericksburg on May 3, as Sedgwick finally began to launch a more spirited attempt. He sent in attacks in the city itself against Lt. Gen. Jubal A. Early's Rebels posted on Marye's Heights, and then the next day drove very deliberately toward Lee's rear. But by now Lee was able to take men from the Chancellorsville line and send them to stop Sedgwick. In and around Salem Church on May 3, Lee stopped the Yankee advance, and the next day himself attacked. Though desultory skirmishing continued over the next two days, Hooker had had enough, and pulled his army back north of the river. The campaign had been a failure, and had gained the North nothing but casualties. The South had once again triumphed, but at terrible cost to herself. For among the thousands she could ill-afford to lose was one of her finest generals, Thomas J. Jackson, who had been shot by friendly forces and later died of complications from his wounds. The debacle had also cost Hooker 17,000 out of his 134,000, while Lee's 61,000-men army suffered 12,800 casualties.

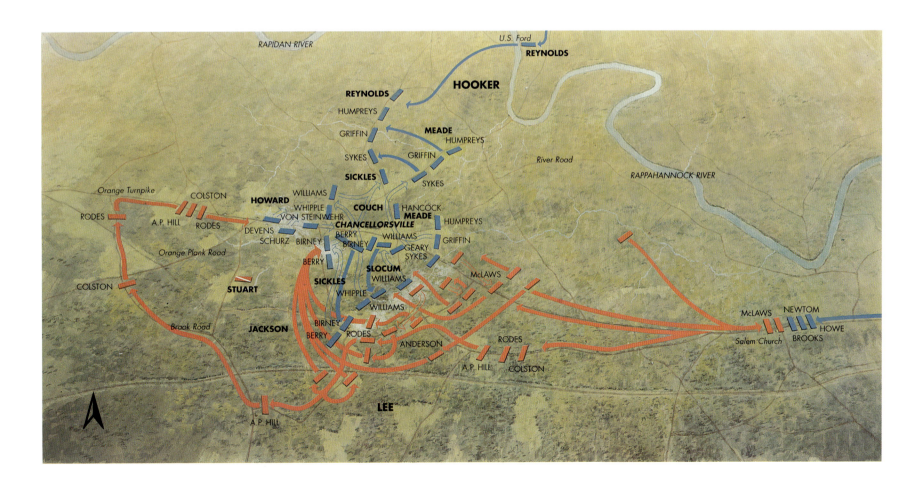

BATTLE OF CHANCELLORSVILLE 221

Private, 140th Pennsylvania Volunteer Infantry, U.S.A.

Private, 69th New York, U.S.A.

LEFT: The 140th Pennsylvania Volunteer Infantry wore standard pattern dark blue tunic, mid-thigh length, over sky blue trousers. The brass shoulder scales were discarded as the war progressed. The longarm was the Belgian-copied French .69 caliber "vincennes" musket, with massive sword-bayonet.

ABOVE: The 69th New York private wore a regulation uniform, largely unornamented: no stripes on trousers, no piping or other color on jacket, and all leatherwork a simple black. The only color was the brass in the beltplate, strap badge, and insignia on the kepi. Nevertheless, the 69th had an enviable reputation.

Private, Co. E, 23rd Virginia Infantry, C.S.A.

Colonel and 1st Lieutenant, 16th Virginia Volunteer Infantry, C.S.A.

ABOVE: The 23rd Virginia Infantryman wore a gray frock coat and trousers, with blue or black trim and distinctive yellow loops on the collars. Leather belt and accouterments were originally white, but hard service quickly soiled them. Some men wore a "B.G." on their kepis, standing for "Brooklyn Grays."

RIGHT: The 16th Virginia Volunteers colonel (standing) wore essentially the regulation field officer's blouse in Confederate gray, with sky blue trousers. The 1st lieutenant wears a similar regulation kepi and trousers, but his blouse is old Federal blue, and he appears to be wearing an old Virginia state beltplate.

BATTLE OF CHANCELLORSVILLE

Seige and Capture of Vicksburg, May 19-July 4, 1863

THE LEADERS

UNION
Army of the Tennessee:
Major General Ulysses S. Grant
Mississippi River Fleet:
Rear Admiral David Dixon Porter

CONFEDERACY
Department of Mississippi and
East Louisiana:
Vicksburg Garrison
Lieutenant General
John C. Pemberton

SIGNIFICANT UNITS

UNION
11th, 20th, 45th, 55th, 72nd,
95th, 99th, 113th and
116th Illinois
83rd Indiana
5th and 12th Iowa
6TH, 8TH AND 11TH MISSOURI
(UNION)
30th, 37th and 53rd Ohio
13th U.S. Infantry
14th and 17th Wisconsin

CONFEDERACY
Arkansas Appeal Battery
20th, 23rd and 30th Alabama
3rd, 21st, 26th and
27th Louisiana
5th and 6th Missouri
(Confederate)
2nd Texas
Waul's Texas Legion

THE SWEEP OF Grant's Vicksburg Campaign is readily evident in the area needed to show his movements. Its beginnings in the intricate series of bayous paralleling the Mississippi in the Louisiana interior appear at upper left. On March 31, 1863, Maj. Gen. John A. McClernand's corps, followed by Maj. Gen. John B. McPherson, began their muddy voyage through these bayous, heading south, sometimes overland, until they emerged on the west bank opposite Bruinsburg, at bottom left. Captain David Dixon Porter's gunboats and transports, meanwhile, had come down the river past Vicksburg's batteries at upper left center. Now these vessels ferried the Yankees across. A week later Sherman's corps made the same journey, and Grant was ready.

He began the overland campaign with a brief sidestep to Grand Gulf to clear it of Rebels, then drove for Raymond, at right center. Defending Confederates stalled him for only a day before he drove on. From here he sent McPherson north to strike the railroad at Clinton, while Sherman and the remainder of McPherson's corps attacked and took Jackson. The state capital fell after two days.

Confederate Lt. Gen. John C. Pemberton, knowing the desperate situation that faced him, moved out of Vicksburg to try to halt Grant's progress. On May 16 he took a position on and around Champion's Hill on the road between Jackson and Vicksburg, at upper right center, but Grant hit him

BELOW LEFT: A portion of the mighty river fleet commanded by David Dixon Porter in the bombardment of Vicksburg. One of the mighty City-class ironclads, originally named *St. Louis*, sits second from left. But by that time her name had been changed to *Baron de Kalb*. She appeared not to be a lucky vessel, having been mauled during an attack on Fort Henry in 1862, and then, after Vicksburg, she struck a mine and sank on July 13, 1863.

hard and drove him from the field. The next day Pemberton tried again at Big Black River Bridge, upper center, but again to no avail. There was now no choice but to pull back into the defenses of Vicksburg itself and hold out, waiting for aid from Johnston that never came.

That same evening Grant moved his first elements up to the defenses, and the next day, May 19, he launched his first assault. It was a spirited and in places desperate affair, but the Confederates held out, as they would through a succession of assaults on subsequent days until Grant finally decided that he would have to lay siege. For the next six weeks the Yankees laid a constant barrage on the beleaguered defenders, meanwhile spreading their lines to close off every avenue of supply or escape. By July 1 Pemberton could hold out no longer. His force was on the brink of starvation and its numbers were decreasing all the time through disease and desertion. Though he hoped until the very end that Johnston would arrive, his position was such that a surrender to Grant's army was inevitable. A meeting between the two commanders on July 3 settled the details of the surrender of the city, which Grant wanted to happen on July 4, a symbolic day for the Union, now to be made the more so. Of Pemberton's army of 28,000, few were casualties but all surrendered. Grant's forces, by contrast, had grown to 77,000 or more.

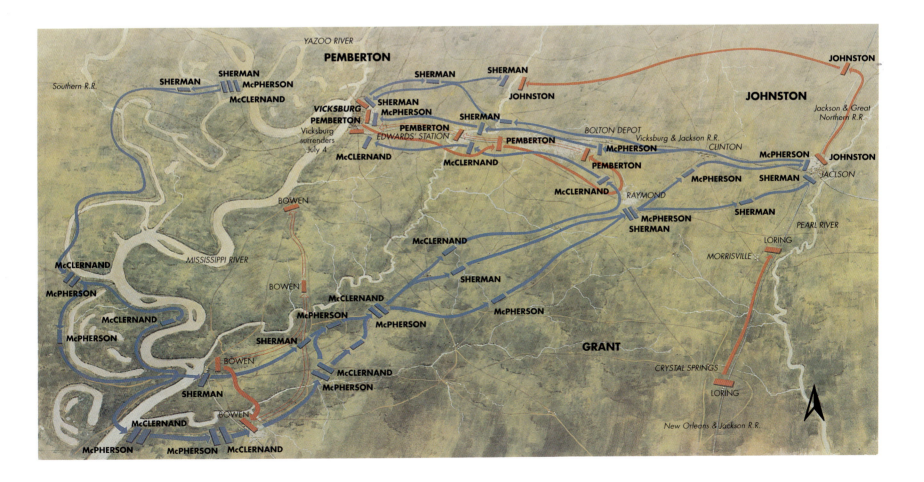

SEIGE AND CAPTURE OF VICKSBURG

Colonel of Engineers, C.S.A.

LEFT: This Confederate engineer colonel wears pretty well standard blouse, trousers, sash, and facings. Indeed, but for his kepi, with its special hat insignia (the "E" in German script), he could easily be a Southern field officer of infantry. Regulations required engineers to wear the chapeau, but they never did.

RIGHT: The Federal commissary sergeant was distinguishable only by his sleeve markings. Otherwise he appeared as any other NCO of the company, although few NCOs could be more important to the enlisted men, since it was from him that they received their food, which they invariably grumbled about.

FAR RIGHT: The 11th Indiana Volunteer Infantry uniform was a Zouave pattern, but in a far from common gray. The jacket was trimmed in red, and obviously not intended for buttoning, since it had no buttons. Even though it was an infantry unit, its officers wore the red shoulder straps normally used by artillery, as did this captain, who also wore a red sash and red piping on the trousers, and gray kepi topped in red. He had buttoned gaiters to gather the cuffs of his baggy Zouave pantaloons to his shoes or boots.

Commissary Sergeant, 30th Ohio Volunteers, U.S.A.

Captain, 11th Indiana Volunteer Infantry, U.S.A.

SEIGE AND CAPTURE OF VICKSBURG

Battle of Gettysburg, July 1-3, 1863 (The First Two Days)

THE LEADERS

UNION
Army of the Potomac:
Major General
George Gordon Meade

CONFEDERACY
Army of Northern Virginia:
General Robert E. Lee

SIGNIFICANT UNITS

UNION
2nd, 6th, and 7th Wisconsin
19th Indiana
24th Michigan
20th Maine
1st Minnesota
69th, 71st, 72nd, and
106th Pennsylvania

CONFEDERACY
13th Alabama
2nd Mississippi
4th, 5th Texas
15th Alabama
9th, 14th, 38th, 53rd, and
59th Virginia

THE FIRST TWO days at Gettysburg were a study in the gradual development of a major battle, as Lee sought to develop a successful attack and Meade sought to counter each move and prepare for the next. Early on July 1 advance elements of the Army of the Potomac first entered the town from the south, and soon discovered A.P. Hill's Confederates approaching from the north and northwest. The Rebels were merely on a foraging raid, but as soon as they first encountered the Federals north of town, at far lower left, they determined to fight. Here in and around McPherson's woods and along the Chambersburg pike, the battle rapidly developed as more and more troops gravitated toward the sound of the guns. Early's division approached from the northwest, upper left, and Maj. Gen. Robert E. Rodes from the north, left center. Meanwhile the Federal I Corps came in on the Fairfield Road, and the Xl Corps rushed up along the Emmitsburg Road, lower right center.

The fighting north of the town became furious. Maj. Gen. John F. Reynolds fell in action, shot dead in the saddle. His subordinate, Abner Doubleday, took command and, despite a brutal punishment inflicted on the Rebels in the Railroad Cut, left lower center, the Federals were finally pushed back through the town in disorder to Cemetery Hill, center. Here, at last, Gen. Winfield Scott Hancock took over and began setting up a desperate line of defenses on the northern and eastern

228 THE BATTLES

BELOW LEFT: The boulders of Devil's Den, Gettysburg, did not ultimately afford enough cover for this Rebel sharpshooter. The story goes that photographer Alexander Gardner, after taking this picture, returned to the spot four months after the epic battle, to find a skeleton in a moldering uniform, the U.S. rifle-musket still propped against the rocks.

slopes of the hill, with his right extending back along the west face to Cemetery Ridge. The first day of the gathering fight came to an end with barely 12,000 Federals remaining of 18,000 who had started.

Reinforcements arrived throughout the night, and by July 2 the armies were substantially complete. Neither Lee nor Meade had planned to give battle over this particular piece of Pennsylvania, but the troops on the ground - and perhaps the hand of fate - had chosen otherwise. Their positions were such that neither could maneuver to another position of their own choosing.

Having both reached the field late on in the day, the commanders of North and South alike spent that first night in reconnaissance and organization of their forces. Both knew that the fight on the following day would be crucial. Fighting did not start until late in the afternoon of the second day, when Lt. Gen. James Longstreet launched his attack on Meade's left and Little Round Top. Maj. Gen. Daniel Sickles had his III Corps injudiciously placed in advance of the Federal line. This made him a perfect Confederate target, and in the Peach Orchard fighting, lower right, the III Corps was almost destroyed. Rebels then moved on to Little Round Top, right center, but spirited resistance held it for the Union. Late that evening another Confederate attack on Cemetery Hill and Culp's Hill, upper left center, also failed.

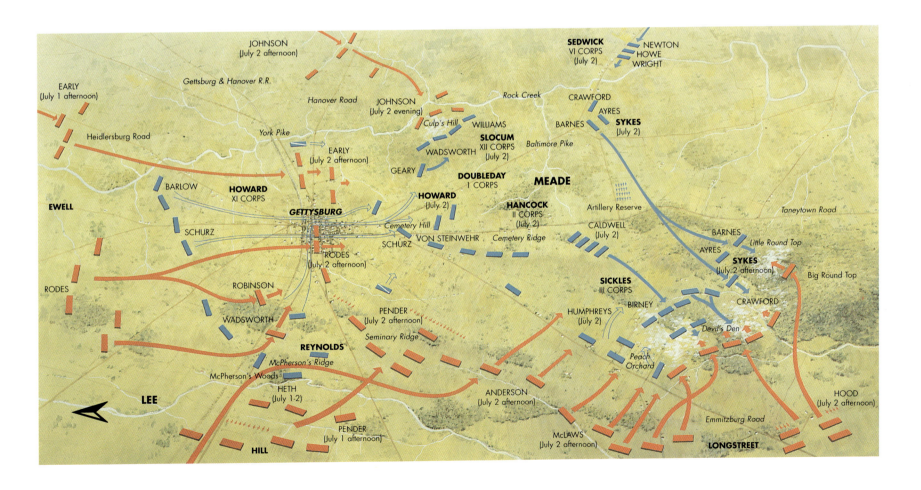

Battle of Gettysburg, July 1-3, 1863 (The Final Day)

All night on July 2, Lee and Meade prepared their armies for what was to come. Meade anticipated that his foe would launch an attack on his center, and heavily strengthened his line and husbanded his reserves. Lee, at the same time, concentrated the mass of his artillery along Seminary Ridge, lower center, intending to batter Meade's center with it before his assault.

When the artillery barrage opened, it aimed at a copse of trees on Cemetery Hill, near right center. But the artillery proved ineffective, largely overshooting the target. Thus, when Longstreet sent forward the Confederate divisions of Generals George E. Pickett and James J. Pettigrew, some 15,000 strong including supports from other commands, the Federal artillery was still in place.

Heroically the Confederates marched across a mile of open ground to rush up the slopes of Cemetery Hill and Cemetery Ridge. As soon as they came in range, they began to take a fearful shelling from Yankee cannon, and then vicious volleys of small arms fire from the bluecoat infantry. Still they pushed on until it came time for the final push. Rushing up the rocky slope of the enemy position, the Rebels flung themselves against men posted behind stone walls and hasty earth and rock mounds. Across a battle front half a mile in width, the struggle became intense. In places, for the first time in the war - and for many their last - men actually engaged in hand-to-hand combat. Yet the

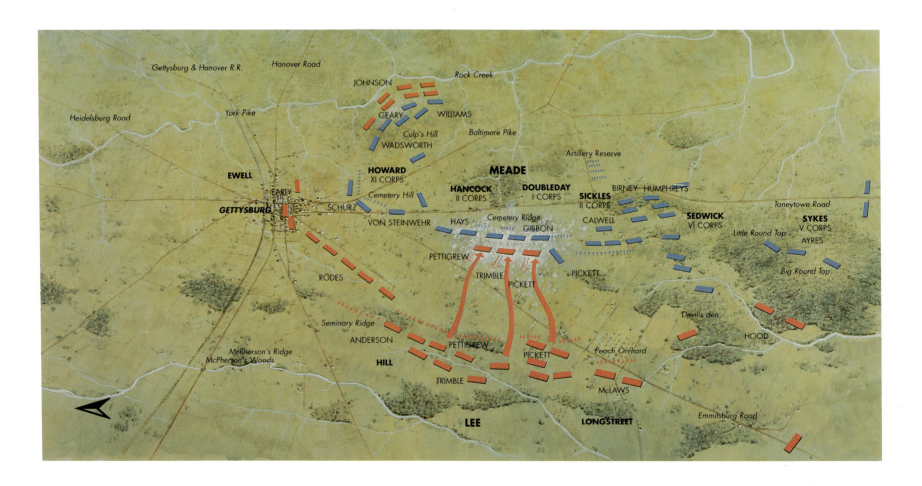

Federals, tough veterans of the II Corps and elements of the old I Corps, held their ground. Only portions of Brig. Gen. Lewis A. Armistead's and Brig. Gen. Richard Brook Garnett's brigades actually penetrated the Federal line, perhaps only 150 in all, and few returned. One of those to get through was General Armistead himself, who got far enough to lay his hand on a Yankee cannon before he was hit.

Inevitably, however, the weight of Union fire and their excellent defensive position told, and the Confederate tide receded toward Seminary Ridge, the grandest frontal assault of the war a failure, and with it Lee's battle. One general lay dead, another mortally wounded, yet another wounded and captured, and nearly half the attacking force killed, wounded or taken prisoner, Other Confederate moves by Ewell's 2nd Corps, and Stuart's cavalry, were also stopped by Federal troops.

On July 4, both armies were too exhausted to do little else but collect their wounded and begin burying their dead. The weather deteriorated towards the end of that fourth day, and under cover of darkness and heavy rain, Lee set the Army of Northern Virginia marching back towards the Potomac and Southern soil. That army's last invasion of the North was over. Many in the North criticised Meade for not pursuing Lee, but the Yankee knew that his army needed time to recover. Gettysburg cost Lee over 20,000 casualties, a fourth of his army. Meade lost 23,000, a fourth of his own.

RIGHT: John Burns's cottage was on the Gettysburg battlefield and, though past seventy years of age, so was he. Seen here with his wife, his crutches and his hunting rifle, he apparently hobbled into the fight, was wounded three times, and is believed to have taken out one or more Confederates who were less than half his age.

Private and Sergeant, 1st Texas Infantry, C.S.A.

15th Virginia Infantry, C.S.A.

LEFT: The 1st Texas early in the war no doubt had gray frock coats and trousers, trimmed with blue, and gray kepis with stars and regimental numerals on the crown. But later they redressed themselves with whatever they could find.

ABOVE: The 15th Virginia was formed in part by amalgamating companies from other regiments. The wounded field officer is helping to support himself with the private's Virginia Manufactory musket converted to use the Maynard tape primer system.

Drummer, Co. F, 2nd Wisconsin Infantry ("Iron brigade"), U.S.A.

Berdan's 1st U.S. Sharpshooters.

LEFT: Berdan's Sharpshooters, armed with .52 caliber Sharps rifles, wore dark green uniform blouses and kepis or hats, with light blue trousers which were later changed to green. These were held to boots with canvas or leather leggings.

ABOVE: Men of the 2nd Wisconsin, part of the famed "Iron Brigade," wore dark blue frock coats and trousers, with the dark Hardee hat, their regimental number encircled by a brass bugle. "The Black Hat Brigade" they were called.

BATTLE OF GETTYSBURG 233

Battle of Chickamauga, September 19-20, 1863

THE LEADERS

Union
Army of the Cumberland:
Major General
William Starke Rosecrans

Confederacy
Army of Tennessee:
General Braxton Bragg

SIGNIFICANT UNITS

Union
44th, 58th and 82nd Indiana
18th, 21st, 40th, 89th and
125th Ohio
17th Kentucky
96th and 115th Illinois
22nd Michigan
39th and 84th Indiana

Confederacy
1st Arkansas
2nd, 15th and 22nd Alabama
3rd and 7th South Carolina
39th and 58th North Carolina
10th Tennessee
65th Georgia
63rd Virginia
5th Kentucky

The Battle of Chickamauga began on September 19 in woods in north Georgia when Federals tried to destroy an isolated Confederate brigade on the west aide of the creek just below Alexander's Bridge, left lower center. However, the battle quickly developed as both sides rushed more and more divisions to the scene, Bragg moving up the east bank of the Chickamauga River, and Rosecrans up the opposite side. Opposing divisions went into line facing each other almost simultaneously, stretching the batteline northward, until it extended almost five miles.

The fighting rolled gradually from the south end toward the center throughout the day. At one point in the afternoon a hole opened in Rosecrans line which, had Bragg taken advantage of it, might have put the Yankees to rout, left center. However, Rosecrans filled it and the fight continued. A substantial attack by Confederate Lt. Gen. Alexander P. Stewart nearly penetrated the enemy line, and later that afternoon a brutal assault by Gen. John Bell Hood on Rosecrans's right flank inflicted serious damage, but the blue line held. The day then closed with a twilight attack by Gen. Patrick R. Cleburne at the opposite end of the field, right center.

Bragg intended a general attack the next day, starting on his right and rolling to the left, the reverse of his Stones River plan. Breckinridge struck first, joined thereafter by Cleburne, and the fury

BELOW LEFT: Part of the battlefield of Chickamauga. On this terriible site and nearby were lost some 16,000 killed, wounded or missing Federal soldiers, and 21,000 Confederates – in just two days of fighting. Put to flight by General Braxton Bragg's forces, the Federal leader, General William S. Rosecrans, soon after fell from grace for effectively fleeing the battlefield, and allowing his troops to be besieged in nearby Chattanooga.

of their assaults led Gen George H. Thomas to call for more and more reserves, especially after Breckinridge pushed around his left flank, center right. Finally Gen. Thomas J, Wood's command pulled out of the center of the Federal line, in obedience to confused orders, opening a massive hole just as Longstreet's men were going in to assault, center left. The effect was electric. The whole Union right collapsed and fled for Chattanooga. The left, commanded by Thomas, pulled back under massive pressure from three sides and held out on Snodgrass Hill long enough to cover the retreat, upper center. Fortuitously, Maj. Gen. Gordon Granger came to his aid from the north, right, and Thomas held out until nightfall. It wasn't until then that Thomas left the field to Bragg. His work had been vital in saving the Federals, for by that time most of the Army of the Cumberland, including Rosecrans, its commander, were well on their way back to Chattanooga.

Bragg now had the chance to completely destroy the Union army, but perhaps partly because of the appalling casualties his force had taken he declined the opportunity. Instead he closed in around Chattanooga. sealed off its lines of supply and began a siege of the Federals inside.

The two-day battle at Chickamauga produced other, more terrible results. Rosecrans lost 16,000 casualties, and Bragg 21,000.

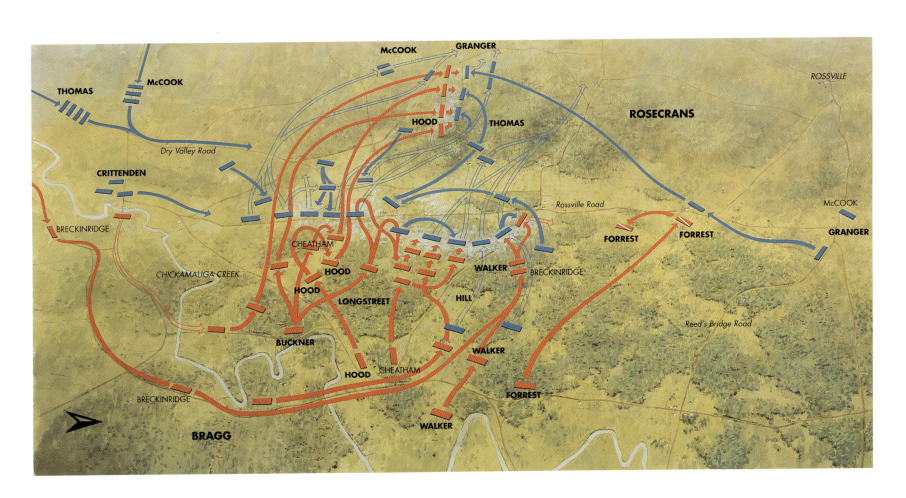

BATTLE OF CHATTANOOGA, NOVEMBER 23-25, 1863

THE LEADERS

UNION
Major General Ulysses S. Grant
Army of the Cumberland:
Major General
George H. Thomas
Army of the Tennessee:
Major General
William T. Sherman

CONFEDERACY
Army of Tennessee:
General Braxton Bragg

SIGNIFICANT UNITS

UNION
46th and 80th Ohio
100th and 103rd Illinois
27th Pennsylvania
5th and 17th Iowa
5th, 6th and 23rd Kentucky
15th, 40th, 51st, 57th and 58th
Indiana

CONFEDERACY
24th, 27th, 29th, 30th and
34th Mississippi
20th Alabama
45th Tennessee
24th Texas Cavalry (dismounted)
Swett's Mississippi Battery
7th, 8th, 9th, 11th and
59th Georgia

GRANT'S BREAKOUT FROM Chattanooga proved to be one of the most spectacular affairs of the entire war. The sheer impressiveness of it all told against the Confederates who supposedly had him bottled up inside the city. During the weeks following the Confederate victory at Chickamauga, Bragg and his army rapidly invested Chattanooga. The city sat with its back to the Tennessee River, at center, and its only usable avenues of retreat or supply were via Brown's Ferry, top center, Tunnel Hill, lower right, or southwestward along the river's south bank, past Lookout Mountain, and then toward Wauhatchie, off the map at top right. Bragg neatly cut off all of these routes by holding the west bank of the river at Brown's Ferry, and by placing his army in a semicircle stretching from Lookout Mountain, upper left center, east to Rosaville, and then along the crest of Missionary Ridge, bottom center, to Tunnel Hill, bottom right center. Additionally, he placed units in the interior north of Chattanooga to cut off any succor to the Northern forces.

To break out, Grant first struck Brown's Ferry in late October, sending units both overland and down the river. With that place secured, a line of supply and reinforcement was open. Next, late in November, when his army was ready, Grant moved forward to Orchard Knob, lower center, on the 23rd to feel Bragg's resistance. The result encouraged him to launch a major assault on Lookout

BELOW LEFT: The view from Lookout Mountain, near Chattanooga. Grant effectively turned defeat into victory when the Confederates, who had gained the upper hand at Chickamauga, but were sorely battered, looked out across the valley and saw the might of the Union army marching upon them. Outnumbered, the Rebels either fell before the Yankee stampede or ran, and this time it was their leader who gave up command.

Mountain the next day. Hooker moved from Brown's Ferry and Wauhatchie and in a spectacular engagement, drove Breckinridge's thin lines from the crest, forcing them back to the main line.

That set the stage for November 25, and the grand assault. Sherman moved across above the city and struck Cleburne and others at Tunnel Hill, where the Rebels stubbornly held on. Then Thomas, first parading his 25,000 men in full view of the enemy, swept forward to the base of Missionary Ridge, and on up its slopes, while Hooker struck Bragg's left flank. The sight of all those Yankees had a demoralizing effect on the men in the lines atop the ridge. Breckinridge's corps was soon put to rout. Whole batteries of artillery were captured, then turned against the remaining defenders. Hardee, commanding the right, suddenly found himself facing Sherman on his front and right, and Thomas on the ridge to his left. He could do no more than hold on for a little while longer until the early winter twilight brought operations to a close. Then he pulled out to join the rest of the shattered army, with the ever defiant Cleburne covering the retreat.

It was the most crushing defeat ever inflicted upon a Confederate army, a fitting revenge for the Yankee loss at Chickamauga. It would also finally make an end of Braxton Bragg as an army commander, and just further impair the noble, ill-fated old Army of Tennessee.

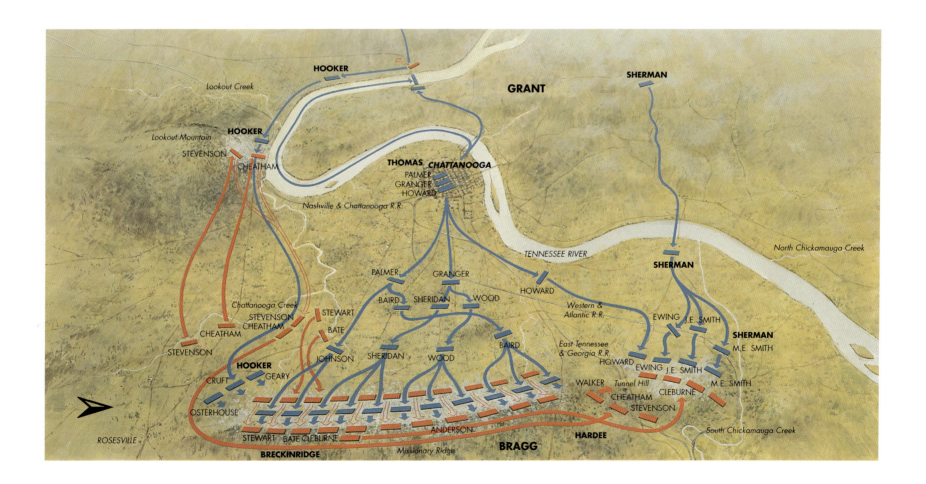

BATTLE OF CHATTANOOGA 237

First Lieutenant, Co. A, 5th Georgia Infantry ("Clinch Rifles"), C.S.A.

Captain, 9th Texas Cavalry, C.S.A.

FAR LEFT: One of the South's most colorful units was the 5th Georgia's Company A, represented by this officer who wore green broadcloth with gilt buttons, and gold lace and trim on the collar and sleeve. His trousers matched, though of a darker green, as did the kepi, on which the letters "C.R." appeared inside a gold wreath. A distinctive feature was the use of U.S. Army insignia for officer rank on shoulder straps instead of on the collar. Two bars meant captain in U.S. service, and 1st lieutenant in the Confederate.

LEFT: This Rebel cavalryman's jacket is gray, trimmed in gold, over brown trousers and brown leather boots, with a distinctive Mexican style of spur. His slouch hat bears a "lone star" inside a circle badge. Weapons are a Dance revolver, a copy of the Colt .44 caliber Dragoon, and an English-made double-barreled shotgun.

RIGHT: Most companies of the 5th Georgia Infantry "Clinch Rifles" wore light blue trousers and dark blue frock coat, as with the corporal at right. As the war ground on the 5th received the standard issue uniform shown at left. Both kepis had the "C.R." insignia, and the men might still have retained their colorful shirts.

5th Georgia Infantry ("Clinch Rifles"), C.S.A.

BATTLE OF CHATTANOOGA 239

Battle of the Wilderness, May 5-6, 1864

THE LEADERS

Union
Lieutenant General
Ulysses S. Grant,
Commander of the Armies
Army of the Potomac:
Major General
George G. Meade

Confederacy
Army of Northern Virginia:
General Robert E. Lee

SIGNIFICANT UNITS

Union
20th Indiana
3rd and 20th Maine
40th, 44th, 86th and 124th
New York
99th, 110th, 118th and
141st Pennsylvania
2nd U.S. Sharpshooters
18th Massachusetts
1st and 16th Michigan

Confederacy
3rd Arkansas
1st, 4th and 5th Texas
18th, 26th, 31st, 38th, 60th and
61st Georgia
15th, 27th, 46th and 48th
North Carolina

Positioned on the south side of the Rapidan River, Lee felt that if he had to stand on the defensive against Grant's forces, although he was outnumbered two to one he still had certain advantages. It was ground he knew better than Grant, and his greatest asset would be the tangled growth of woodland and bush known locally as the Wilderness, crossable by only a few roads. Running across the center, from left to right, is the Orange Turnpike. The Orange Plank Road, coming up from the southwest, intersects at right center, at Wilderness Church and Dowdall's Tavern. The Germanna Plank Road comes in from the north to meet the Turnpike at the Wilderness Tavern, center, where Wilderness Run crosses it. The Brock Road connects the Orange Plank Road and the Turnpike at center, while the Ely's Ford Road comes in from the north at right center to Chancellorsville.

Meade had sent Hancock down from Ely's Ford toward Chancellorsville, while Maj. Gen. Gouverneur K. Warren's V Corps and Sedgwick's VI Corps moved on the Germanna Plank Road. When it became apparent that Lee would meet them before they could march through the Wilderness, Meade turned Warren west to meet Lt. Gen. Richard S. Ewell's rushing Confederates along the Turnpike, left center. Hancock, meanwhile, began to move west toward Lee's flank, bottom center, and Sedgwick came up on Warren's right. While Warren was attacking Ewell, Hill's Corps

BELOW LEFT: Men of the 44th New York, who were to fight in the horrific but indeterminate Battle of the Wilderness, camped near Alexandria, Virginia, for an extended period in early 1864. Most of their time was devoted to rest and preparations for the epic battles to come under their commander, Ulysses S. Grant, newly appointed general-in-chief of all Union armies, in his pursuit of Lee. However, the soldiers did take the trouble to let passers-by know the number of their unit and some of the engagements in which they had taken part.

rapidly approached on the Plank Road from the lower left, and Hancock arrived on the scene just in time to help blunt the Confederate thrust at Warren's left flank. During the rest of the day there were essentially two battles, Ewell against Warren and Sedgwick on either side of the Turnpike, and Hancock against Hill on the Plank Road. Neither proved decisive.

The next day, May 6, Grant planned a major assault, but Lee struck first, hitting Sedgwick's right flank. The attack failed, but soon thereafter Longstreet's providential arrival on the Plank Road slammed into Hancock and soon put Hancock's left in serious jeopardy, bottom center. By noon, Longstreet had pushed around Hancock, seriously endangering the whole Federal position. Even Burnside's late arrival between Hancock and Warren did not stem the Gray tide, lower center. But Lee's army was spent by this time and could not sustain the momentum any longer. By this time, Grant had also decided that this particular battle had run its course. Darkness was falling, and it was clear that a decisive result was now beyond his reach. However, Grant had crossed the river to fight and take the war to the Confederacy. Northern Virginia was where the war was, and Grant intended his army to stay there. The stage was being set for that long struggle that was to end at Appomattox. Lee lost 8,7000 of his 63,000 men, but he held Grant's 120,000 and inflicted 17,000 casualties.

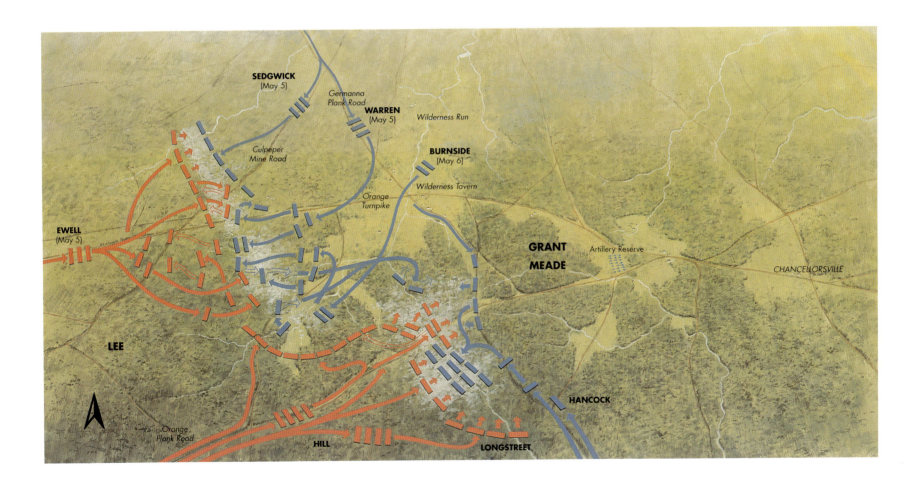

BATTLE OF THE WILDERNESS 241

Officer, 39th New York Volunteer Infantry ("Garibaldi Guard"), U.S.A.

Officer and enlisted man, 83rd Pennsylvania Volunteer Infantry, U.S.A.

FAR LEFT: Revealing a strong European influence, the men of the 39th New York Volunteers adopted association with Garibaldi, an Italian hero of the time, hence "Garibaldi Guard." Most distinctive uniform feature is the plumed hat with chin strap. Unlike most Yankee officers, he carries no shoulder straps as insignia of rank, and has piping of gold on his shoulder seams.

LEFT: Probably no Federal regiment presented a more mixed bag of elements in its private soldiers' costume than the 83rd Pennsylvania Infantry. The enlisted man, foreground, wears a cap such as that seen with Scottish Highlanders, and sports epaulets normally worn only by general officers, a somewhat shortened blouse similar to that worn by some Zouaves, and exceptionally baggy Zouave pantaloons. The lieutenant, by contrast, wears entirely standard uniform.

RIGHT: The basic uniform of the 4th Texas Volunteers showed some variations from the regulation Confederate pattern. Most noticeable was the black piping, rather than blue. Headgear reflected more what was available than prescribed for, from the slouch hat of the kneeling man, foreground, to the modified top hat or prewar Hardee hat on the sergeant. The lone star of Texas decorated their hats and sometimes beltplates.

Enlisted men, 4th Texas Volunteer Infantry, C.S.A.

BATTLE OF THE WILDERNESS

Battle of Fort Fisher, December 25, 1864, January 13-15, 1865

THE LEADERS

Union
Department of Virginia and North Carolina, Terry's Provisional Corps:
Brevet Major General Alfred Howe Terry
North Atlantic Squadron, U.S. Navy:
Rear Admiral David Dixon Porter

Confederacy
Department of North Carolina:
Major General Braxton Bragg
Wilmington and Cape Fear District:
Major General William Henry Chase Whiting
Fort Fisher Garrison Commander:
Colonel William Lamb

SIGNIFICANT UNITS

Union
3rd, 47th, 48th, 112th, 117th, 142nd New York
76th, 93rd, 203rd Pennsylvania
Naval and Marine Brigade

Confederacy
36th North Carolina State Troops (2nd North Carolina Artillery)
Detachments of 11th, 21st and 25th South Carolina
Detachments of naval and marine units

THE FINAL ASSAULT of Fort Fisher was the climatic event of a campaign that began in November 1864 as a novel if impractical idea in the fertile mind of Union Major General Benjamin F. Butler. It became a joint venture of the North Atlantic Blockading Squadron commanded by Rear Admiral David Dixon Porter and Army units commanded by General Butler. The objective was to close the last open port of the Confederacy on 3,549 miles of southern coastline at Wilmington, North Carolina. The port was guarded by a mammoth L-shaped sand fortification with a northern land face 430 yards wide and a sea face three-quarters of a mile long. Fifty cannon were mounted, among them fifteen heavy Columbiad smoothbores and a 150 pounder 8-inch English Armstrong rifle. The fort was manned by 1,400 North and South Carolinians and Naval and Marine Detachments under the direct command of Colonel William Lamb.

Butler had 6,500 men from units of the XXIV and XXV Corps, Army of the James, supported by a fleet of almost 60 naval warships including 30 monitor-class ironclads. The plan was to float a shallow draft powder ship, the 143-foot-long *Louisiana* loaded with 430,000 pounds of powder, close to the fort and detonate it. Butler expected the force of the blast to level the fortification and enable his assault troops to walk ashore. His plans went awry from the beginning. There was total lack of coordination and cooperation between Army and Navy counterparts. The ship was finally anchored too far off the fort and detonated early Christmas Eve morning with no noticeable effect. Butler aborted his assault the next day, leaving 700 assault troops under the fort's guns. Lieutenant General U. S. Grant replaced bumbling Butler with Major General Alfred H. Terry who, with Porter,

developed a new plan of attack. On January 13 three divisions of white soldiers and one division of U.S. Colored Troops established a beachhead above the fort's land face. On January 14 forty-four ships of Porter's squadron commenced a concentrated naval bombardment and, at 4:00 p.m., he sent his naval and Marine contingent of 2,000 men against the northeast salient of the sea face. At the same time three brigades under Colonels Newton Martin Curtis and Louis Bell and Brigadier General Galusha Pennypacker stormed the land face. By 9:00 p.m. the fort was taken.

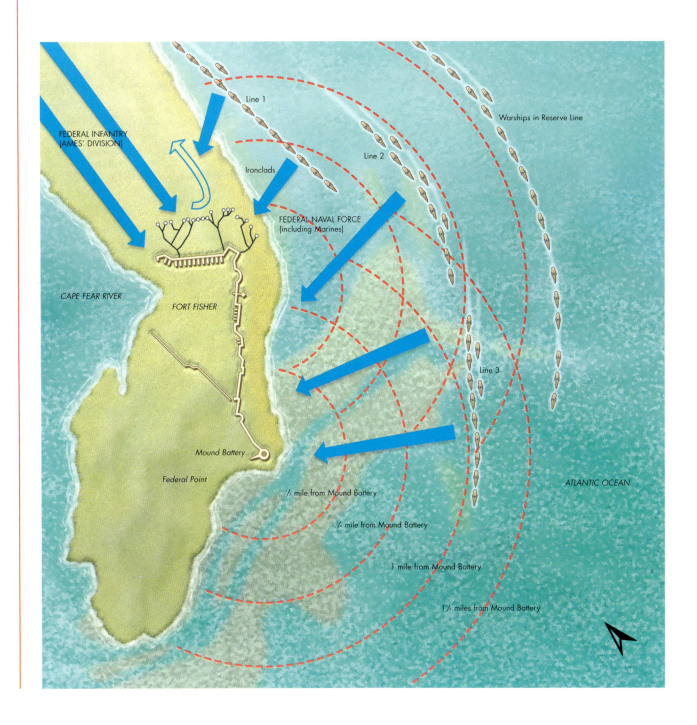

LEFT: Fort Fisher, North Carolina, as seen in 1865, with a view of the first traverse, northwest end, showing entrance to the fort. The Federal attack, involving elements of the Army, Navy and Marines, was a debacle, its plan being described by future Admiral George Dewey as "sheer, murderous madness," because the naval officers entrusted with the operation had no experience with amphibious operations or assault tactics.

BATTLE OF FORT FISHER 245

Private, U.S. Colored Infantry.

Private, Washington Light Infantry, C.S.A.

246 THE BATTLES

FAR LEFT: Tens of thousands of ex-slaves were enlisted in more than 100 all-black regiments, though initially they were regarded more as laborers than combat soldiers. Uniforms and equipment were mainly standard issue, as in this view of an infantryman who took part in the attack on Fort Fisher, but it wasn't until a few months before this assault that black soldiers received as much pay as their white comrades.

LEFT: The Washington Light Infantry, whose "WLI" badge is clearly shown on this private's kepi, served in and around Charleston, S.C., after Fort Sumter, and then in July 1863 was merged into the 25th South Carolina Infantry. The regiment was later captured at Fort Fisher.

RIGHT: The Union Navy lieutenant at left wears the optional white trousers with his dark blue tunic, and white service hat. The first lieutenant of Marines wears a uniform similar to that of the Army, chief differences being in the insignia and gold lace around the collar.

Lieutenant U.S.N. and First Lieutenant U.S. Marine Corps

BATTLE OF FORT FISHER 247

Battle of Nashville, December 15-16, 1864

THE LEADERS

UNION
Department of the Cumberland:
Major General
George H. Thomas

CONFEDERACY
Army of Tennessee:
General John Bell Hood

SIGNIFICANT UNITS

UNION
114th Illinois
93rd Indiana
10th Minnesota
72nd and 95th Ohio
17th, 18th and 44th U.S.
Colored Troops

CONFEDERACY
1st and 3rd Florida
1st, 2nd, 5th, 13th and
15th Arkansas
2nd, 10th, 20th and
37th Georgia
4th Georgia Sharpshooters

NASHVILLE SAT INSIDE a bend of the Cumberland River, approached by a series of roads leading west, south, and east. Most important in the Confederate approach to the city, and the subsequent retreat, were the Nashville Pike, top center, the Franklin Pike just below it, the Granny White Pike below that, and the Hillsboro Pike, below that, along which Hood constructed his left flank defenses, when he determined that his intent to attack was impracticable. Thomas, meanwhile, had erected his own perimeter of defenses just outside Nashville's limits, left center, and later made a second, outer line of works on his center and right, covering the Granny White and other routes to its west.

When Hood's offensive stalled, and when winter and his own hesitation allowed, Thomas planned an offensive of his own. On December 15 he sent Maj. Gen. James H. Wilson and his cavalry out to clear the Charlotte Pike of enemy cavalry, bottom center, and then to start a sweep around Hood's left flank. At the same time, Gen. A.J. Smith and Gen. Thomas J. Wood (the same general whose strict obedience to an order led to the rout at Chickamauga) moved out to strike the Confederate defenses along the Hillsboro Pike, where sharp fighting broke out, lower center. Meanwhile, Gen. James Steedman advanced against Hood's right behind Brown's Creek near the Nashville Pike. Heavily outnumbering his foe, Thomas had the battle almost all his own way all day, and Hood was forced to

pull back to a hastily erected new line that night between the Franklin and Hillsboro Pikes.

Here Thomas struck him again on December 16, and this time decisively. Steedman swept down on Lt. Gen. Stephen D. Lee on Peach Orchard Hill, top right, Wood and Smith struck the center under A.P. Stewart, and Gen. John Schofield turned Hood's left flank under Gen. Benjamin Franklin Cheatham on Shy's Hill, lower right. Wilson, meanwhile, almost completed the envelopment, riding into Cheatham's rear. Faced with such an overwhelming force on three sides, Hood's army simply started to melt away as the threat of being surrounded became evident.

More troops began to turn and run for the Franklin Pike. A few heroic rearguard actions, particularly one made by Hood's small cavalry force, held off the Federals long enough for the battered Army of Tennessee to make good an escape, but the army by that time was in such chaos that its officers could not even make reports as to how many of their men were left dead on the field. Meanwhile Thomas continued to attack. The Confederate's retreat was one long rearguard action fought out under the most appalling conditions. Only after they had crossed the Tennessee did Thomas stop the pursuit. By the end, Hood lost 5,500 or more, forty percent of his army of 24,000. Thomas, by contrast, lost only 3,000 of his 50,000 engaged.

BELOW LEFT: The Tennessee state capitol, located on the top of a hill in Nashville, had defending guns virtually on the steps of the building when it was under siege in December 1864. The conquering Union army soon set about building a lengthy railroad trestle bridge which would facilitate movement of its troops and supplies.

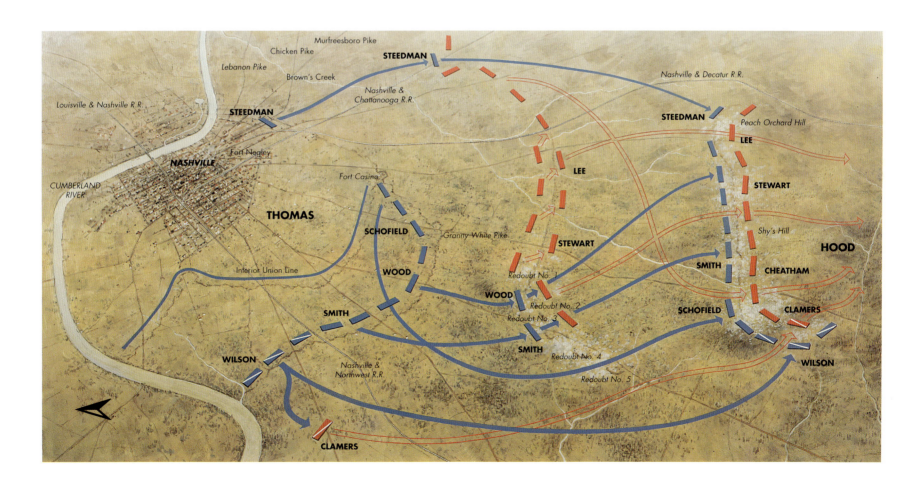

Private (and mascot) of the 8th Wisconsin Volunteer Infantry, U.S.A.

LEFT: Quite a number of regiments went to war with special mascots, including little drummer boys, vivandiers (women in military costume), and most of all pets. Dogs, cats, raccoons, even small bears, went to war, but no mascot was as distinctive as "Old Abe," the "war eagle" that accompanied the 8th Wisconsin Infantry of the old Iron Brigade across the battlefields of Tennessee and Georgia. His tenders wore mainly regulation uniform, except that their headgear was more likely to be the slouch hat.

ABOVE RIGHT: Maj. Gen. George H. Thomas achieved success at Nashville over a weakened Army of Tennessee. He lost very few men, but captured many rebels and their valuable equipment.

ABOVE, FAR RIGHT: By contrast, General John B. Hood's career was ended at Nashville. Humiliated, he asked to be relieved in January, and thereafter saw no active service.

RIGHT: Once this trestle bridge had been erected in a remote region near Whiteside, Virginia, a constant stream of traffic poured along the Nashville and Chattanooga Railroad, a vital transport link for the Federal forces.

INDEX

Page numbers in **bold** refer to captions for illustrations.

A

accouterments, Federal
    miscellaneous 116, **116-117**
    see also equipment; leather accouterments and equipment
Anderson, Maj. Robert 192
Antietam, Battle of 206-207, **206-207**
arbor, brush-covered "shebang" **127**
Armistead, Brig. Gen. Lewis A. 231
arsenals, Confederate 151-152
arsenals, Federal 148, 150-151
artillery 36
    Confederate 34
    Federal 34, 213
artillery battery, light **9**
artillery units, reenacting 31
"Authentic Campaigner, The" website 21-22
authentic items 26, **28**

B

badges, Federal corps 82, **82-83**
    see also insignia, Federal
balloons, observation 36
band, Confederate regimental **178**
band leader's baton, Federal **118**
bands, Federal military 118, 120
Barlow, Col. Francis S. **134**
Baron de Kalb **225**
Bartow, Col. Francis 194
battles 190-193
Bayne, Capt. N. **83**
bayonet frogs and scabbards, Federal 110, **110-111**
bayonet scabbard, Confederate **148**, **153**
bayonets 29
    Confederate **148**, **153**, 174, **175**
    Federal **89**, **110**, **111**
Beall, First Lt. John A. **49**
Beauregard, Gen. Pierre G. T. **128**, **133**, 182, **184**, 194, 199
Beaver Dam Creek, battle at 202
bedroll, Federal **114** *see also* blankets, Federal
bedrolls 29
Bee, Brig. Gen. Bernard 194
belt plates, Confederate 142-143, **142-143**

belts, waist 28 *see also* sword belts
    Confederate 140-141, **140-141**
    Federal **39**, **110**
        enlisted men's 87, **87**
        officers' 86, **86**
        sergeants' **59**
Berwyn Rod and Gun Club, Maryland 19
Big Bethel, battle at 192
binoculars, Federal 116, **117**
black powder safety 19, **31**
blankets, Federal 116, **117** *see also* bedroll, Federal
blouses, Confederate uniform **128**, **129** *see also* shirts, Confederate
boots *see* footwear
Brady, Matthew **189**
Bragg, Gen. Braxton **128**, 214, 215, 216, **219**, 234, 235, 236, 237
Brandy Station, Va **39**
Breckenridge, Gen. John C. 215, 216-217, **217**, 234-235
Brewster, Lt. Henry M. **48**
brigadier general, Federal **109**
Buckner, Lt. Gen. Simon Bolivar **128**, **130**, **134**
Buell, Maj. Gen. Don Carlos 199
bugles, Confederate **179**
bugles, Federal **118**, **119**, **120**
Bull Run, First Battle of (First Manassas) **3**, 194-195, **194-195**
    reenactment 19
Bull Run, Second Battle of (Second Manassas) 203
bullet molds, Confederate 168, **168**
Burns, John 231
Burnside, Gen. Ambrose 206-207, 210, 211
Burton, Capt. Charles **50**
Butler, Maj. Gen. Benjamin F. 244
buttons, Confederate 144-145, **144-145**
buttons, Federal 41, 84-85, **84-85**

C

Camp Chase Gazette 31
campsite 30
canteens 28-29, **30**, 35
    Confederate 176, **176**, **177**
    Federal 59, 114-115, **114**
cap boxes, Confederate 166-167, **166-167**

cap boxes, Federal 102, 104, **104**, 110
caps *see* headgear
captains, Confederate
    infantry **34**
    Tennessee Light Artillery, 1st **201**
    Texas Cavalry, 9th **239**
    Virginia Infantry, 11th (Lynchburg Home Guard) **213**
captains, Federal
    Artillery, U.S. **34**
    Indiana Volunteer Infantry, 11th **226**
cartridge boxes, Confederate 148, 166-167, **166-167**, 168
cartridge boxes, Federal 102, **102-103**
cartridges 12
cartridges, Confederate 168
Cassals, Maj. John **83**
cavalry, Confederate **34**
cavalry horse equipment 22 *see also* saddles, Federal
cavalry units, reenacting 31
cavalrymen, Federal **10**, **106**
Chancellorsville, Battle of 220-221, **220-221**
character, taking on 29
Charleston Harbour, South Carolina 191, 192
Chase, Capt. Benjamin **135**
Chattanooga, Battle of 236-237, **236-237**
Chickamauga, Battle of 234-235, **234-235**
Citizen's Companion 31
City Point cemetery, Virginia **190**
Civil War Canteens 28
Civil War News 19, 30
civilians, reenacting 31
Clark, Col. W. J. **136**
Clasby, Robert **22**
Cleburne, Gen. Patrick R. 234-235
Clem, Little Johnny **201**
coats, Confederate 24
    1861 Regulation 128
    enlisted men's 137, **137**
    frock 130-131, 137, **137**
    Navy 131
    officers' 128-131, **128-132**
    sack 137
coats, Federal 24
    chasseur 60
    enlisted men's 54-61, **54-56**, **58**, **61**

    frock 40-41, 54, 57
        officers' 40-41
    officers' 40-43, **40-41**, **43**
    overcoats, enlisted men's 30, **61**
    sack **56**, 57
        officers' 41
Cobb, First Sgt. Harlan **67**
Coleman, Capt. Lindley M. **50**
colonel, Federal, 16th Virginia Volunteer Infantry **223**
colonels, Confederate **27**
    artillery **34**
    of engineers **226**
colors *see* flags
Colt, Samuel 94, 97
Colt Patent Firearms Company 94
Confederate States of America 191
Confederate units
    Alabama Volunteer Corps **143**, **145**
    Army of Northern Virginia 16
    Army of the Tennessee **185**
    Carolina Rifles, 1st, Orr's Regiment **204**
    "Dixie Rangers" **181**
    Florida Volunteer Infantry, 1st and 3rd (combined) Regiments **187**
    Florida Volunteer Infantry, 3rd, Florida Independent Blues, Co. B **181**
    Georgia Infantry, 5th, Co. A ("Clinch Rifles") **239**
    Georgia Infantry, 44th **204**
    Georgia Regiments, 7th and 8th **134**
    Georgia Volunteer Infantry, 57th Regiment **186**
    Kentucky Brigade, 1st ("Orphan Brigade") **185**
    Kentucky Infantry, 4th ("Orphan Brigade") **201**
    Kentucky Infantry, 6th **180**
    Mississippi, 9th **127**
    Mississippi Infantry, 11th **209**
    Mississippi Volunteer Infantry, 7th Regiment **187**
    North Carolina, 26th **178**
    North Carolina Infantry Regiment **183**
    South Carolina Volunteer Infantry, 5th Regiment, Co. B **182**
    South Carolinians, Kershaw's Brigade 16

Tennessee Cavalry, 6th Battalion **136**
Tennessee Infantry, 16th **187**
Tennessee Light Artillery, 1st **201**
Texas, 1st **232**
Texas, 4th **135**
Texas, Van Dorn Guards **184**
Texas Cavalry, 8th ("Terry's Texas Rangers") **218**
Texas Cavalry, 9th **239**
Texas Volunteer Infantry, 4th **243**
Virginia, 6th **135**
Virginia, 13th Battalion, Co. A **136**
Virginia, 22nd, Co. B **135**
Virginia Cavalry Regiment, 1st **197**
Virginia High Constabulary, Courtney's **184**
Virginia Infantry
   11th (Lynchburg Home Guard) **213**
   15th **232**
   23rd, Co. E **223**
   45th, Co. B (F) **135**
Virginia Light Artillery, 13th Battalion, Co. A **169**
Virginia Partisan Rangers, 43rd **27**
Virginia Volunteer Infantry regiments
   7th **182**
   8th **184**
   9th **185**
   16th **223**
Washington Artillery **213**
Washington Light Infantry **247**
Cook and Brother **152-153, 156**
corporal, Confederate, 5th Georgia Infantry, Co. A ("Clinch Rifles") **239**
Crittenden, Maj. Gen. Thomas L. **214-215, 216, 217, 217**
Cumberland Landing, Virginia **203**

D
Davis, Jeff **48**
decorations, Confederate **146-147**
decorations, Federal enlisted men's **76**
decorations, Federal officers' **74**
Dempsey, Henry L. **13**
Dillingham, Captain **44**
Doubleday, Abner **228**
drill, light artillery battery **9**
drummer, Federal, Co. F, 2nd Wisconsin Infantry ("Iron brigade") **233**
drums, Confederate snare **179**
drums, Federal snare **119, 121**

E
Eisenhower, Dwight D. **190**
engineers, Confederate **226**
enlisted men, Confederate **243**
   see also privates, Confederate; trooper, Confederate
epaulets, Confederate **146-147**
epaulets, Federal officers' **78, 79, 80**
equipment **12-13** *see also* accouterments, Federal miscellaneous; leather accouterments and equipment
equipment, purchasing **21-22**
Evans, Brig. Gen. Nathan **194**
Ewell, Lt. Gen. Richard S. **240, 241**

F
Fair Oaks, battle at **202**
Fayetteville arsenal, North Carolina **151-152**
Federal units
   Army of the Potomac **203**
   2nd Army Corps, 2nd Division **124**
   Army of the Tennessee **201**
   Artillery, U.S. **34**
   Berdan's 1st U.S. Sharpshooters **35, 42, 70, 233**
   Cavalry, 1st U.S. **39**
   Cavalry, 4th U.S. **53**
   Colored Infantry, U.S. **247**
   Connecticut Infantry, 10th **48**
   Corps, II **211**
   Corps, III **229**
   Illinois Volunteers **70**
   Indiana Volunteer Infantry, 11th **226**
   Maine Infantry, 19th **50**
   Marines, U.S. **247**
   Massachusetts Battery, 4th **49, 75**
   Massachusetts Battery, 10th **52**
   Massachusetts Heavy Artillery, 2nd **211**
   Michigan, 4th **27**
   Minnesota, 1st **22**
   Navy, U.S. **247**
   New Hampshire Volunteer Infantry, 2nd **213**
   New Jersey Cavalry, 3rd (the "Butterflies") **57**
   New York Cavalry, 11th ("Scott's 900") **57**
   New York Infantry regiments
      5th (Duryee's Zouaves) **51, 204**
      8th **75**
      9th (Hawkins' Zouaves) **61, 63, 209**
      12th, Co. I **11**
      22nd **33**
      44th **241**
      57th **48**
      69th **222**
      79th ("Highlanders") **197**
      137th **113**
      143rd **50**
      146th **15**
   New York National Guard **58, 71**
      7th Regiment **68**
      50th Regiment **68**
   New York State Militia, 7th **71, 113**
   New York State Militia, 50th **71**
   New York Volunteer Infantry, 9th, Co. C **67**
   New York Volunteer Infantry, 39th ("Garibaldi Guard") **23, 75, 243**
   Ohio Infantry, 94th **49**
   Ohio Volunteers, 30th **226**
   Pennsylvania Artillery, Ementrout's Independent Company **53**
   Pennsylvania Artillery, Independent, Battery F **52**
   Pennsylvania Cavalry
      1st, Bayards Brigade **83**
      1st, Co. G **124**
      6th ("Rush's Lancers") **56, 60, 204**
      6th, Co. E **76**
      6th, Co. I **125**
      13th, Co. G **53**
      19th **83**
   Pennsylvania Infantry
      5th **41**
      23rd (Birrey's Zouaves) **59, 63**
      95th (Gosline Zouaves) **61**
      118th **82**
   Pennsylvania Reserves, 13th Regiment **75**
   Pennsylvania Volunteer Infantry
      56th **122**
      62nd, Co. H (Zouaves) **119**
      76th, Co. B ("Keystone Zouaves") **67, 73**
      83rd **70, 243**
      91st **124**
      99th **122**
      114th ("Collis' Zouaves") **53**
      114th, Co. F **70**
      138th **123**
      140th **222**
   Rhode Island Infantry, 2nd **197**
   Sheridan's Cavalry Corps **83**
   Vermont Infantry **44**
   Veteran Reserve Corps **56**
   Wisconsin Infantry, 2nd, Co. F ("Iron Brigade") **233**
   Wisconsin Volunteer Infantry, 8th **250**
firearms tools and accessories *see also* cartridge boxes
   Confederate **165, 168-169, 168-169**
   Federal **104-105, 104-105**
   see also pouch for percussion caps
Fish, Pte. Latham Avery **67**
flags, Confederate
   battle **180, 180, 182, 185-186**
   National **180, 181, 182, 184**
   unit **181-187, 219**
flags, Federal national and unit **122-125, 122-125**
Floyd, Brig. Gen. John B. **141**
foot soldier, Federal, Army of the Tennessee **201**
footwear
   boots **22-23, 24**
      Confederate **139, 139**
      Federal **72, 73, 73**
   brogans **22-23, 24**
      Confederate **3, 139, 139**
      Federal, Pattern 1851 Jefferson **72**
   Confederate **139, 139**
   Federal **72-73, 72-73**
Fort Fisher, Battle of **244-245, 244-245**
Fort Monroe, Virginia **191**
Fort Pickens, Florida **191**

Index

Fort Sumter, South Carolina 191-192
Fowler, Lt. Col. William **15, 43, 51**
Franklin, Gen. William B. 210
Fredericksburg, Battle of **189**, 210-211, **210-211**
Freeman, G. W. 119
Funk, Col. Augustus 75
fuze pouch and belt, Federal artillery 117

G
Gaines' Mill, battle at 202
Gardner, Alexander 229
Gardner, Maj. Gen. Frank **131**
generals, Confederate **217, 219, 251**
generals' uniforms, Federal **40, 44**
Gettysburg, Battle of 228-231, **228-231**
    Cemetery Hill 228, 229, 230-231
    charge of the 1st Minnesota 22
    Devil's Den 229
    reenactments
        125th Anniversary 16, **17,** 19
        McPherson's Ridge **7, 23**
        Pickett's Charge **15**
Glendale, battle at 202
Goodman, Lt. Samuel **82**
Goodrich, Lt. William **83**
Gorgas, Col. Josiah 153
Gracie, Brig. Gen. Archibald Gracie, Jr. **173**
Granger, Maj. Gen. Gordon 235
Grant, Gen. Ulysses S. **44**, 198-199, **199**, 224-225, 236-237, 241, **241**
Grayson, Capt. A. J. **135**
grenades, hand 36
ground cloth, rubberized 29, 35
gunners, Confederate, Washington Artillery **213**

H
Hamilton, Capt. Paul **134**
Hancock, Gen. Winfield Scott 228-229, 240, 241
Hardee, William J. 48, 237
hats *see* headgear
haversack, personal items in 13, **13,** 29-30
haversacks, Confederate 176, **176**

haversacks, Federal 112, **112**
headgear, Confederate 24-25
    caps
        enlisted men's 138, **138**
        officers' 133-136, **133-136**
    chapeaus 133-134, **135**
    forage caps (kepi), Confederate 133, **133,** 134, **134, 135,** 136, 138, **138**
    hats
        camp 136
        enlisted men's 138, **138**
        Hardee 134
        officers' 133-136, **133-136**
        rain, rubberized 135
    havelock, cotton 135
    headwarmer, wool 135
    slouch hats 133,134, 136, 138, **138**
    civilian 134, 136
headgear, Federal 24-25, **26**
    caps, chasseur 48, **50,** 71
    caps, enlisted men's 66-71, **66, 69,** 71
    chapeaus 47, 51-52
    fezzes, Zouave **67,** 70
    forage caps **1, 68**
        colonel's **82**
        lieutenant colonel's, 146th New York Regiment **15**
        M1858 (kepi) 46, **46,** 47, 48, **50-51,** 52, 53, 66
        Pattern 1861: 66, 68
    hats
        Albert style, Model 1851: **68**
        enlisted men's 66-71, **67-71**
        Hardee or Jeff Davis 48, 50, 66, **67,** 70
        rain, patent rubber **70**
    havelock cap ("whipple hat") **49**
    havelocks **11,** 68, 70
    kepis (havelocks) **11**
    officers' 46-53
    shakos **68,** 70
    Federal Light Artillery 47, 66
    slouch hats 46, 47, 48, **50-51, 53**
    civilian 70
Henry, Mrs. 195
Herring, Col. (later Brevet Brig. Gen.) Charles P. **82, 83**

Hill, Lt. Gen. Ambrose Powell 207
Historic Graphics **22**
Hobson, Capt. J. **169**
holsters, Confederate **161, 168, 169**
holsters, Federal 105
Homan, 2nd Lt. Levi J. **53**
Hood, Lt. Gen. John Bell **129, 130,** 186, 234, 248-249, **250**
Hooker, Gen. Joseph ("Fighting Joe") 220, 221, 237
horse equipment 22 *see also* saddles, Federal
Howard, Maj. Gen. Oliver O. 195
Hunley, CSS 36
Huse, Caleb 153-154

I
identification disks 35
identity, taking on 29
infantry, Confederate 34
insignia 40 *see also* buttons
    Confederate braid, gold sleeve (galloons) 131-132, 147
    Confederate collar 132
    Federal 35 *see also* badges, Federal corps
        branch and unit, enlisted men's 76-77, **77, 189**
        branch and unit, officers' 74, **74-75**
    rank
        Confederate 131-132, 146-147, **146-147**
        Federal officers' 78-81, **78-81**
ironclads, City-class **225** *see also* ships, armored

J
jackets, Confederate
    enlisted men's 137, **137**
    officers' 128-131, **128-132**
    shell 25-26, 130-131, 137, **137**
jackets, Federal
    enlisted men's 54-61, **55-61**
    officers' 40-43, **42, 43**
    shell 56, 57-58, **57**
    New York State 58, **58**
    officers' 42
    Zouave 60
Jackson, Gen. Thomas Jonathan "Stonewall" **133,** 195, 202, 220, 221

Johnston, Gen. Albert Sydney 198
Johnston, Gen. Joseph E. 202

K
Kinchloe, First Lt. W. James **136**
Kirkpatrick, W. H. **135**
knapsack, personal items in 13, **13,** 29-30
knapsacks, Federal 112-113, **113, 114**

L
Latta, Brevet Maj. James W. **83**
leather accouterments and equipment 27-28
Lee, Hutson **132**
Lee, Gen. Robert E. **133,** 206, 207, 210, 220, 221, 229, 230, 240
    Seven Days' Battles 202, **203,** 203
leggings, Federal 73
lieutenant, Confederate, Orr's Regiment, 1st Carolina Rifles **204**
lieutenant, second, Federal, 5th New York Infantry **204**
lieutenant colonel, Confederate, 44th Georgia Infantry **204**
lieutenants, Federal 27, **109**
    U.S. Navy **247**
lieutenants, first
    Confederate, Georgia Infantry, 5th, Co. A ("Clinch Rifles") **239**
    Federal
    Marine Corps, U.S. **247**
    New York Infantry Regiment, 9th ("Hawkins' Zouaves") **209**
    Rhode Island Infantry, 2nd **197**
    Virginia Volunteer Infantry, 16th **223**
Lincoln, Abraham 191
Linton, Maj. Samuel S. **49**
Longstreet, Lt. Gen. James 229, 230, 241
Louisiana 244

M
Maffatt, Capt. J. N. **33**
Magruder, Brig. Gen. John B. **134**
major, Confederate cavalry 34
major generals, Federal **215, 217, 251**

Mallorie, Cpl. Walter H. **51, 67, 73**
Malvern Hill, battle at 203
Manassas, Battle of First (First Bull Run) 3, 194-195, **194-195**
  reenactment 19
Manassas, Battle of Second (Second Bull Run) 203
Manassas battlefield 193
marches 8
mascots **250**
McClellan, Maj. Gen. George Brinton 202-203, **203**, 206
McDowell, Brig. Gen. Irvin 194
McHenry, Capt. Alexander H. **53**
McPherson, Maj. Gen. John B. 224
Meade, Maj. Gen. George G. **40, 46, 73, 78**, 210, 229, 230, 231, 240
mess gear, Federal 114, 115, **115**
Militia Act, 1808: 148, 160
monocular glass, Federal 116, **117**
Mosby, John Singleton "Gray Ghost" 27
Murfreesboro, Battle of 214-217, **214-217**
musical instruments and equipment, Confederate 178, **178-179**
musical instruments and accouterments, Federal 118-121, **118-121**
musicians, Federal **120**

N
Nashville, Battle of 248-249, **248-249**, 251
National Parks 30
neck socks, Federal enlisted men's **65**, 65
nightcap **13**
North-South Skirmish Association (NSSA) 19

O
officers, Federal **243**
ordnance, Federal 35-36
ordnance industry, Confederate local 163-164
Otey, Captain G. Gaston **136**, **169**

P
Palen, First Lt. Peter **50**
Parker, Lieutenant 27
Paxon, Private Thaddeus **70**
Pemberton, Lt. Gen. John C. 224-225
percussion caps, Confederate **165**
percussion caps, Federal 104
personal items 13, **13**, 29-30, 112-113
Pierce, Capt. Charles P. **48**
plate, CSA **127**
Polk, Gen. Leonidis 215
Porter, Captain (later Rear Admiral) David Dixon 224, 244
pouch for percussion caps, Federal sergeant's **59**
powder flasks, Federal **105**
Prentiss, Maj. Gen. Benjamin 198
privates, Confederate *see also* enlisted men, Confederate; trooper, Confederate
  Kentucky Infantry, 4th **201**
  Mississippi Infantry, 11th **209**
  Texas, 1st **232**
  Virginia Infantry, 15th **232**
  Virginia Infantry, 23rd, Co. E **223**
  Washington Light Infantry **247**
privates, Federal *see also* foot soldier, Federal
  Artillery, U.S. **34**
  Colored Infantry, U.S. **247**
  New Hampshire Volunteer Infantry, 2nd **213**
  New York Infantry Regiment, 9th ("Hawkins' Zouaves") **209**
  New York, 69th **222**
  Pennsylvania Volunteer Infantry, 140th **222**
  Wisconsin Volunteer Infantry, 8th **250**
publications 19, 26-27, 28, 31

R
Railroad, Nashville and Chattanooga **250**
Randolph, Brig. Gen. George Wythe **131**, **133**
Reenacting, War Between the States, as a hobby 17-18
  history of 19
reenacting artillery units 31
reenacting cavalry units 31
reenacting civilians 31
reenactment group, joining 19-20
reenactments **16, 17, 20, 21**
reenactors, types of 20, **22**
Regulations, 1851: 65, 86, 87
Regulations, 1858: 54
Regulations, 1861: 54, 62, 65, 86
Remington, E., and Sons 97-98
research, uniforms 25-27
Reynolds, Maj. Gen. John F. **228**
Richmond 193
Richmond Armory 151, 156
Rodman, Isaac P. 207
Rosecrans, Gen. William S. 214, 234, **235**
Rosser, General **129**
Rothermel, Lt. J. A. **83**

S
saddles, Federal 116, **116**
safety 19, **20, 21, 31**
St. Louis 225
sashes, Federal officers' 78, 80
scabbards, Confederate **170-173**, **174, 175**
  bayonet **148, 153**
scabbards, Federal 110, **110-111**
Schofield, Gen. John 249
Sedgwick, Maj. Gen. John **47**, 220, 221
Semmes, Brig. Gen. Paul **130**, **134**
sergeants, Confederate
  Texas, 1st **232**
  Texas Cavalry, 8th ("Terry's Texas Rangers") **218**
sergeants, Federal
  commissary, 30th Ohio Volunteers **226**
  New York Infantry, 79th ("Highlanders") **197**
  Pennsylvania Cavalry, 6th ("Rush's Lancers") **204**
Seven Days' Battles 202-203, **202-203**
Seven Pines, battle at 202
sewing kit, Federal "housewife" **13**, 112
Sharpsburg, Battle of 206-207, **206-207**
Sharpshooters, Federal, Berdan's 1st U.S. **233**
shelter half 35
Sheridan, Maj. Gen. Philip H. 214, **215**
Sherman, Brig. Gen. William T. **40**, 198, 237
Shiloh, Battle of 198-199, **198-199**
ships, armored 36 *see also* ironclads, City-class
shirts 23-24, **25**
  Confederate **137** *see also* blouses, Confederate uniform
  Federal enlisted men's 64-65, **64, 65**
shoulder straps, Federal officers' 78, 79, **80**
Sickles, Maj. Gen. Daniel **229**
skirmishes 19
Sleeper, Capt. J. Henry **52**
Smith, Gen. A. J. 248, 249
Smithsonian Institution 25
spurs, Federal 73, 116, **117**
Starr Arms Company 98
State Parks 30
Steedman, Gen. James 248, 249
Stewart, Lt. Gen. Alexander P. 234
Stones River, Battle of 214-217, **214-217**
Stuart, Maj. Gen. J. E. B. **133**, **159**, 195
Sumner, Brig. Gen. Edwin V. **109**
Sumner, Lt. Samuel S. **109**
sutlers (suppliers) 20-21, 22, 27, 28
sword belt, Federal cavalry enlisted man's **5**
sword belts, Confederate 140

T
Taylor, Lt. George W. **49, 75**
Taylor, Maj. Robert B. **135**
Tennessee River 199
tents, Confederate **127**
tents, Federal A frame **33**
Terry, Maj. Gen. Alfred H. 244-245
Thomas, Maj. Gen. George H. 235, 237, 248, 249, **250**
Tigress 199
training 19
trooper, Confederate, 1st Virginia Cavalry Regiment **197**
trousers, Federal 24
  enlisted men's 62, **62-63** *see also* leggings, Federal officers' 44, **44, 45**
  Zouave 62
Tyler, Brig. Gen. Daniel 194, 195

U
underclothes 23
uniform, purchasing 21-22

Index

uniforms, Confederate 11, 12, 25-26
    butternut-colored 34
    material 132, 137
uniforms, Federal 11-12, 25, 35
uniforms, research 25-27
utensils, Federal eating 13

V
Vicksburg, siege and capture of 224-225, **224-225**

W
waistcoat, Confederate 25-26
Wallace, Maj. Gen. Lew 199
Warren, Maj. Gen. Gouverneur 51
Warwick, Col. Bradflute 135
Washington 192
water bottles, Confederate 176, 177 *see also* canteens
weapons *see also* firearms tools and accessories; grenades, hand
    reproduction 29
    rocket launcher, Hale's patent 36
weapons, Confederate 10-11
    carbines, cavalry 156-159, **156-159**
        Bilharz, Hall and Company **158**, 159
        British Pattern Enfield 157
        British Terry's Pattern 1860: **156**
        Calisher and Terry 159
        Cook and Brother 159
        Dickson, Nelson and Company **156**
        Keen Walker and Company **158**
        Le Mat 157
        Morse 158
        Murray, J. P. 156
        Richmond 159
        Robinson, S. C., Sharps **158**
        Tallahasee 157
        Tarpley 157
    edged 170-175, **170-175**
        knives, side 174, **174-175**
        sabers 170-173
        swords 171-173
    imported from England 153-154, 162-163
    musketoons **150**, 151
    muskets 148-155
        Morse smoothbore muzzle-loading 152
        Palmetto Armory Model 1842 smoothbore 151
        State of Georgia smoothbore muzzle-loading alteration 153
        Virginia Manufactory 232
    pistols 10, **161**, **162**, 163, 165
    revolvers 160-165, **160-165**
        British Beaumont-Adams 161
        British Kerr **160**, 162
        British Tranter **160**, 161
        British Webley double action, .44 caliber 160
        Clark, Sherrard and Company 165
        Cofer, T. W. 164
        Colt .44 Dragoon 219
        Colt Model 1848, 3rd Model 160
        Colt Model 1860 Army 161-162, **169**
        Colt Navy .36 caliber 10
        Columbus Fire Arms Mfg Company 164
        Dance, J. H., and Brothers **163**, 239
        French manufactured pinfire 160
        Griswood and Gunnison **162**, 164
        Le Faucheaux 163
        Le Mat 33, 163, **164**, 165
        Leech and Rigdon 37, **162**
        Remington New Army 161
        Rigdon, Ansley 162
        Spiller and Burr 162
        Tucker, Sherrard and Company 164
        Wilson & Leavitt Army 160
    rifle-muskets 148-155
        British pattern 1853 Enfield 148
        Richmond muzzle-loading, late model 155
    rifles 148-155
        Belgian pattern short 148
        British Brunswick 149
        British Kerr's Patent 149
        British Pattern 1842 short 148
        British Whitworth Patent, with telescopic sight 150
        Chapman, C., muzzle-loading 154
        Cook and Brother muzzle-loading 155
        Davis and Bozeman muzzle-loading 152
        Dickson, Nelson and Company muzzle-loading 151
        Fayetteville 149, **152**
        Lamb, H. C., muzzle-loading 155
        Mendenhall, Jones and Gardner muzzle-loading 152
        Murray, J. P., muzzle-loading 154
        muzzle-loading 153
        Pulaski, muzzle-loading 155
        Read and Watson late model muzzle-loading 155
    shotgun, English-made double-barreled 239
weapons, Federal 9-10, 11
    carbines 91-92
        Burnside .54 caliber **92**, 92
        Gallagher percussion 92, **92**
        Joslin 93
        Maynard 93
        Merrill 93
        Sharps 10
        Smith .50 caliber **92**, 93
        Spencer .52 caliber **92**, 93
        Starr 93
    edged 106-109, **106-109**
        cutlasses 106
        sabers 10, 106, **106**, 107, **108**, 109, **109**
        swords 106, **106**, 107, **108**, 109, **109**, 120, 197
    muskets **88**, **88-89**, 222
    pistols 101
    revolvers 94-101
        Allen & Wheelock Lipfire Army, .44 caliber 100
        Butterfield Percussion Army, .41 caliber 99
        Colt Army 9, 10, 94, **97**, 97, 98, 101, 197
        Colt Model 1849 Pocket 98
        Colt Model 1851 Navy 94, 97
        Colt Model 1862 Police 96
        Freeman Army Model, .44 caliber 101
        Joslyn Army, .44 caliber 99
        Le Faucheaux 101
        Manhattan Pocket Model 96
        Massachusetts Arms Company Adams Patent Navy 94
        Perrin and Company, .45 caliber 96
        Pettengill Army, .44 caliber 99
        Plant Third Model 96
        Remington 95
        Remington-Beals Navy 95
        Savage Navy 98
        Savage-North Navy, .36 caliber 100
        Smith & Wesson 37, 97
        Starr 95, **98**, **99**, **100**
        Whitney Navy 96, 98
    rifle-muskets 88-89, **88**, 91, **91**
    rifles 89-90
        .58 caliber 9
        Enfield .577 caliber 9
        Greene 90
        Henry 35, **89**, 90
        Jenks Navy 90
        Model 1841: **88**, 89-90
        Model 1855: 89, 90
        Sharps 90, 91, **92**, 233
        Spencer 35, **36**, 90, **90**
Webb, Second Lt. George W. 52
websites 19, 21-22
Weitzel, Brig. (later Maj.) Gen. Godfrey 26
Wheeler, Maj. Gen. Joseph 130
White, Capt. Selleck L. 48
Wilderness, Battle of the 240-241, **240-241**
Wilson, Maj. Gen. James H. 248, 249
Wister, Capt. Langhorne 75
Wood, Gen. Thomas J. 248, 249
Wright, Capt. William A. 141

Y
Yorke, Col. P. J. 83

Z
Zoaves 11, 30